Full E   nt

Full Employment: The Elusive Goal

Derek H. Aldcroft

Professor of Economics
University of Leicester

Wheatsheaf
Books

Distributed by Harvester Press

First published in Great Britain in 1984 by
WHEATSHEAF BOOKS LTD
A MEMBER OF THE HARVESTER PRESS PUBLISHING GROUP
Publisher: John Spiers
Director of Publications: Edward Elgar
16 Ship Street, Brighton, Sussex

© Derek Aldcroft, 1984

British Library Cataloguing in Publication Data

Aldcroft, Derek H.
  Full employment
  1. Labor supply — Great Britain
  2. Unemployment — Great Britain
  I. Title
  331.13′7941   HD5765.A6

  ISBN 0-7108-0293-5

  ISBN 0-7108-0298-6 Pbk

Typeset in Times 11 on 12 point by
Alacrity Phototypesetters,
Banwell Castle, Weston-super-Mare.
Printed in Great Britain by
Butler & Tanner Ltd, Frome and London

THE HARVESTER PRESS PUBLISHING GROUP
The Harvester Press Publishing Group comprises Harvester Press
Limited (chiefly publishing literature, fiction, philosophy, psychology,
and science and trade books), Harvester Press Microform Publications
Limited (publishing in microform unpublished archives, scarce printed
sources, and indexes to these collections) and Wheatsheaf Books Limited
(a wholly independent company chiefly publishing in economics,
international politics, sociology and related social sciences), whose books
are distributed by The Harvester Press Limited and its agencies
throughout the world.

Contents

Preface   vii

1   Unemployment Patterns in the 1930s and 1980s   1

2   Unemployment and Economic Policy   21

3   Economic and Financial Constraints to Fiscal
    Action   37

4   Technical Change, Structural Transformation
    and Jobless Growth   63

5   Problems of Regional Imbalance   94

6   The Constraint of Inflation   127

Conclusion: The End of Full Employment   157

Index   162

Preface

This book attempts to explain why it is so difficult to get back to full employment in conditions of severe and prolonged unemployment as in the 1930s and at the present time. As far as it is practical, a comparative analysis is made between the two periods. Chapters 1 and 2 provide the background material to the unemployment problem, the economic conditions and the policy dimensions of the two periods in question, while the core of the book, Chapters 3–6, discuss the main constraints in the way of achieving full employment. The essay does not specifically deal with the causes of unemployment, nor does it pretend to have found a final solution to the problem. However, while it argues that there is no quick and viable way of curing unemployment, the concluding chapters offer some advice on policy action.

My grateful thanks go to Mrs Margaret Christie for expertly typing the draft chapters, with some assistance from Mrs Gillian Austen.

Derek H. Aldcroft
University of Leicester

1 Unemployment Patterns in the 1930s and 1980s

Despite imperfections in the unemployment statistics, there can be little doubt that throughout most of the inter-war period, and especially in the 1930s, unemployment was the central economic problem. Virtually all the major industrial countries suffered severely in the early 1930s as a result of the sharp contraction in economic activity after 1929, though several were already experiencing employment difficulties in the previous decade, partly as a result of the distortions caused by the aftermath of the war. The standardised unemployment percentages in Table 1.1 not only illustrate the marked increase during the early 1930s but also point to the fact that even by the end of the decade unemployment was still running well above the levels of the 1920s and those before 1914, though the inadequacy of the statistical base for the earlier period makes precise comparisons impossible. On average, unemployment in the 1930s was more than twice as high as in the previous decade.[1] Moreover, the numbers involved were anything but small; at the depth of the slump in 1932/3 over 3 million were out of work in Britain, 6 million in Germany and some 13 million in the United States. Even these figures do not tell the whole story since there were many more living on reduced incomes as a result of under-employment.

If anything the re-emergence of unemployment as a major issue in recent years has been more traumatic than in the earlier period since it followed a period of very full employment. Apart from the post-war reconstruction period through to the mid-1950s when some countries, such as Germany, Italy, Belgium and Denmark, were still recording fairly high un-

TABLE 1.1 Unemployment as a Percentage of the Total Labour Force, 1920-38

	Austria	Belgium	Denmark	Germany	Netherlands	Norway	Sweden	UK	USA
1920	—	—	3.0	1.7	1.7	—	1.3	1.9	3.9
1925	6.3	0.9	7.5	3.0	2.4	3.4	2.6	7.7	3.8
1929	5.5	0.8	8.0	5.9	1.7	5.4	2.4	7.2	3.1
1930	7.0	2.2	7.0	9.5	2.3	6.2	3.3	11.1	8.7
1931	9.7	6.8	9.0	13.9	4.3	10.2	4.8	14.8	15.2
1932	13.7	11.9	16.0	17.2	8.3	9.5	6.8	15.3	22.3
1933	16.3	10.6	14.5	14.8	9.7	9.7	7.3	13.9	20.5
1934	16.1	11.8	11.0	8.3	9.8	9.4	6.4	11.7	15.9
1935	15.2	11.1	10.0	6.5	11.2	8.7	6.2	10.8	14.2
1936	15.2	8.4	9.5	4.8	11.9	7.2	5.3	9.2	9.8
1937	13.7	7.2	11.0	2.7	10.5	6.0	5.1	7.7	9.1
1938	8.1	8.7	10.5	1.3	9.9	5.8	5.1	9.2	12.4

Source: A. Maddison, *Phases of Capitalist Development* (1982), p. 206.

employment levels, rates of unemployment in the major industrial economies, with the exception of the United States, averaged around 2 per cent or less. From the middle of the 1960s there was a gradual drift upwards through to the early 1970s after which unemployment rates moved up sharply in all countries apart from Switzerland. As the figures in Table 1.2 demonstrate, by the early 1980s unemployment was on average three to four times greater than in the mid-1960s, with the UK recording a double figure rate by 1981. At the time of writing unemployment shows little sign of marked improvement and it is still increasing in some countries.

TABLE 1.2: **Standardised Unemployment Rates in Fifteen OECD Countries (percentage of labour force) 1966-81**

	UK	*7 Major Countries* [1]	*EEC Total* [2]	*OECD Total* [3]
1966	2.2	2.6	2.3	2.5
1967	3.3	2.8	2.8	2.7
1968	3.3	2.9	3.1	2.8
1969	3.0	2.7	2.7	2.5
1970	3.1	3.2	2.7	3.0
1971	4.0	3.8	3.0	3.5
1972	4.2	3.8	3.3	3.6
1973	3.2	3.4	3.0	3.2
1974	3.1	3.7	3.1	3.5
1975	4.7	5.5	4.5	5.2
1976	6.1	5.5	5.2	5.3
1977	6.5	5.4	5.5	5.3
1978	6.4	5.1	5.5	5.2
1979	5.7	5.0	5.6	5.1
1980	7.3	5.6	6.0	5.8
1981	11.4	6.5	8.0	6.8

Notes: 1 Canada, USA, Japan, France, Germany, Italy, UK
2 Belgium, France, Germany, Italy, Netherlands, UK
3 Countries in 1 and 2 above, plus Australia, Austria, Finland, Norway, Spain, Sweden

Source: OECD, *Labour Force Statistics*, Quarterly Supplement, 1982 (3), p. 77.

Full Employment: The Elusive Goal

In both periods Britain fared badly on a comparative basis. Her unemployment was well above the general average of other major countries in both cases while her economy was fundamentally weak, more particularly in the later period. Moreoever, Britain's current unemployment rates (11-12 per cent) are not far removed from those recorded in the worst years of the inter-war depression (12-15 per cent), while the total volume of unemployment at 3 million plus is almost identical to that of the early 1930s. Because of distortions in the data, these figures may not necessarily reflect the true position,[2] but the magnitudes are sufficiently large to leave little doubt as to the severity of the problem both in the 1930s and the 1980s.

A breakdown of employment trends by sector gives some indication as to where jobs were being lost, and in this respect there are some interesting differences between the two periods. Employment in industry and manufacturing reached a peak in the middle of the 1960s and since then it has declined almost continuously. In total over 4 million jobs have been lost in industry, some three-quarters of them coming from manufacturing. The decline in employment opportunities gathered pace during the 1970s under the influence of the disturbed economic conditions of that decade, and in recent years the decline has averaged about 8 per cent per annum, as against 2 per cent in the late 1960s and early 1970s. Most other countries have experienced stagnation or contraction in industrial employment during recent years but not to anywhere near the extent as in the UK.[3] The extent and severity of the decline in manufacturing employment has prompted a lively debate on the question of whether Britain is undergoing a process of de-industrialisation.

Perhaps even more remarkable is the widespread incidence of employment losses. Every major sector in the standard industrial classification order has experienced a drop in employment since the middle of the 1960s, as the figures in Table 1.3 demonstrate. In some cases the decline has been very steep indeed. Between 1966, the peak year in manufacturing employment, and June 1982 many branches of industry suffered a contraction in employment of one-third or more, and in two cases, metal manufacture and clothing and footwear, it has exceeded 50 per cent. Mining, construction and gas, electricity and water also experienced a hefty drop in numbers employed. The shake-out in manufacturing has therefore been widespread and it has affected prosperous as well as stagnating industries. Indeed, during the 1970s and early 1980s some of the most flourishing concerns, GEC, Racal, Beecham and Hawker Siddeley, were shedding labour along with their weaker brethren.[4] A combination of high wage costs, slack market conditions, and technical improvements, encouraged, and forced in some cases, many firms to rationalise and improve the efficiency of their operations.

TABLE 1.3 **Employees in Employment in Great Britain, 1966-82 (mid-year estimates, 000s)**

		1966	1982	% change 1966-82
1	Agriculture, forestry, fishing	464.1	346	-25.5
2	Mining and quarrying	574.2	325	-43.4
3	Food, drink and tobacco	832.1	605	-27.3
4	Coal and petroleum products		26	
5	Chemical and allied trades	524.6	388	-21.1
6	Metal manufacture	622.6	294	-52.8
7	Mechanical engineering		724	
8	Instrument engineering	2 347.7	129	-36.4
9	Electrical engineering		640	
10	Shipbuilding and marine engineering	200.1	140	-30.0
11	Vehicles	845.2	547	-35.3
12	Metal goods	596.0	428	-28.2
13	Textiles	757.3	298	-60.5
14	Leather, leather goods and fur	59.2	29	-51.0
15	Clothing and footwear	527.6	260	-50.7
16	Bricks, pottery, glass and cement	361.0	204	-43.5
17	Timber, furniture, etc.	314.1	203	-35.4
18	Paper, printing and publishing	644.1	493	-23.5

5

		1966	1982	% change 1966-82
19	Other manufacturing industry	344.9	236	-31.6
20	Construction	1 636.6	1 011	-38.2
21	Gas, water, electricity	422.9	329	-22.2
22	Transport and communications	1 609.3	1 372	-14.8
23	Distributive trades	2 925.6	2 653	-9.3
24	Insurance, banking, finance and business services	638.8	1 305	+104.3
25	Professional and scientific services	2 512.5	3 650	+45.3
26	Miscellaneous services	2 196.0	2 484	+13.1
27	Public administration and defence	1 344.3	1 497	+11.4
3-19	Total manufacturing industries	8 976.4	5 644	-37.1
2.21	Total production industries	11 610.1	7 308	-37.1
22-27	Total service industries	11 226.5	12 960	+15.4
1-27	All industries and services	23 300.7	20 614	-11.5

Sources: Department of Employment and Productivity, *British Labour Statistics: Historical Abstracts 1886-1968* and *Department of Employment Gazette.*

Had it not been for continued expansion in the services sector as a whole, the unemployment situation would have been very much worse. And even in this sector there was contraction in two major categories, transport and communications and the distributive trades. However, to offset these there was very rapid expansion in insurance, banking and finance, and in professional and scientific services, with lesser gains in miscellaneous services and public administration and defence. Public sector employment as a whole recorded one of the largest gains during the period; the total numbers engaged in the public sector rose from 5.4 to just over 7 million between 1961 and 1978 and by the latter date it was almost as large as manufacturing.[5] However, despite the buoyancy of the service sector, by the mid-1970s the scope for further job creation was beginning to wane especially since after this date there was some tightening up of recruitment in the public sector. Overall, therefore, the net loss of jobs in the economy had exceeded 2½ million by the middle of 1982 (see Table 1.3).

The trends in employment demonstrate quite clearly therefore the widespread nature of the losses in jobs in the last decade or so, and currently very few sectors are actively recruiting additional workers. In the inter-war years, by contrast, the job losses were rather more heavily concentrated in particular sectors of the economy; although employment, both at the aggregate and sectoral levels, fluctuated somewhat more from year to year with the trough in total employment being recorded in 1931, there was, thanks partly to the strong recovery in the 1930s, a net increase in employment for the period as a whole. Between 1920 and 1938 the total number of persons employed rose by 5½ per cent, while the losses recorded in the manufacturing and production sectors of the economy were very modest compared with more recent trends (see Tables 1.3. and 1.4). While it is true there was a substantial contraction in several branches of industry – notably in mining, textiles, metal manufacturing, engineering and shipbuilding, where employment fell by between one-quarter and one-third – there was more or less an equal number of manufacturing activities which were experiencing a growth in employment. These included food, drink and tobacco, electrical goods, vehicle manufacturing, building materials and paper, printing and publishing, most of which not only recorded substantial gains in numbers employed over the inter-war period as a whole, but were also employing more workers than ever before at the trough of the employment cycle in 1931. At the same time building and contracting and gas, electricity and water registered very significant gains in employment, whereas latterly both sectors have been contracting. Again however, the main employment growth occurred in the services sector with very strong expansion in most branches apart from public administration and transport and communications. Overall, service sector employment rose by 20 per cent during the inter-war years as against a contraction of 2-3 per cent in manufacturing and industrial production.

TABLE 1.4: **Total Persons in Employment by sector 1920-38 (000s)**

		1920	*1931*	*1938*	*% change 1920-38*
1	Agriculture, forestry and fishing	1 741	1 425	1 272	-26.9
2	Mining and quarrying	1 325	958	904	-31.8
3	Food, drink and tobacco	619	642	767	+23.9
4	Chemical and allied trades	253	214	274	+8.3
5	Iron and steel	541	258	357	-34.0
6	Mechanical engineering and shipbuilding	1 313	544	882	-32.8
7	Electrical goods	188	212	337	+79.3
8	Vehicles	353	443	623	+76.5
9	Other metal goods	515	395	532	+3.3
10	Textiles	1 331	1 001	1 007	-24.3
11	Clothing	896	776	814	-9.2
12	Bricks, pottery, glass, cement	209	231	298	+44.0
13	Timber, furniture, etc.	323	280	322	-0.3
14	Paper, printing, publishing	393	435	492	+25.2
15	Leather and other manufacturing industries	274	228	265	-3.3
16	Building and contracting	927	1 008	1 266	+36.6
17	Gas, water, electricity	185	238	291	+57.3
18	Transport and communications	1 641	1 558	1 692	+3.1
19	Distributive trades	2 352	2 778	3 090	+31.4
20	Insurance, banking, finance	369	410	475	+28.7
21	Professional services	845	958	1 115	+32.0
22	Miscellaneous services	2 307	2 663	3 110	+34.8

		1920	1931	1938	% change 1920-38
23	Public administration and Defence	1 397	1 010	1 233	-11.7
	Central government	257	186	245	-4.7
	Local government	380	499	556	+46.3
	Armed forces	760	325	432	-43.2
3-15	Total manufacturing industries	7 208	5 659	6 970	-3.3
2-17	Total productive industries	9 645	7 863	9 431	-2.2
18-23	Total service industries	8 911	9 377	10 715	+20.3
1-23	Total all industries and services	20 297	18 665	21 418	+5.5

Source: C. H. Feinstein, *National Income, Expenditure and Output of the United Kingdom 1855-1965* (1972), Table 59, T129-30.

On balance, therefore, the incidence of employment contraction has been very much more widespread through the economy in recent years. The total net loss of jobs has not only been far greater, but it has affected a far larger number of industries and sectors, with the total absence of any expanding sectors in manufacturing in contrast to the situation between the wars. This contrast between the two periods is again reflected in the unemployment data which show a much stronger occupational and geographical concentration in the earlier period. The production industries accounted for a very large share of total unemployment in the inter-war years. In 1929 and 1933 some 45 per cent of all unemployment was accounted for by the manufacturing sector, and nearly three-quarters by the production sectors (manufacturing plus mining, construction and gas, electricity and water), whereas these two groups were responsible for only 30 and 40 per cent respectively of total employment. By comparison, in May 1981 manufacturing's share of total unemployment was 30.7 per cent and 47 per cent for the production industries as a whole, though their shares of total employment were somewhat less than in the early 1930s.

9

The aggregate figures however do not fully reflect the heavy industrial concentration of unemployment in the inter-war years since much of it was located in the former big staple industries which had flourished during the ninteenth century. As a result of technical changes and shifts in demand patterns these industries suffered a sharp and permanent contraction in the demand for their products, especially from overseas. They were also relatively inefficient, overmanned industries and when market conditions became difficult after the war they were forced to shed labour rapidly. Thus in the first half of the 1920s employment in mining, shipbuilding, textiles, engineering and metal manufacture fell by more than 1 million. These five large groups, with a share in total employment of some 18 per cent, accounted for nearly one-half of the total unemployment in 1929 and 46 per cent in 1933. If building and public works and the distributive trades are added to the list, then some two-thirds of the unemployment can be accounted for by seven main sectors of activity.[6] Moreover, as we shall see, the high geographic concentration of the staple industries posed an acute problem for the northern regions of the country.

The position is somewhat different in the early 1980s. There are no overwhelming concentrations of unemployment, either industrial or geographic, in manufacturing as was the case in the inter-war years. It is true that manufacturing activities as a whole have suffered badly in respect of job losses, but unemployment in each individual branch of manufacturing accounts for a relatively small part of total unemployment; in fact the highest share of total unemployment is that of mechanical engineering at 4 per cent (May 1981). By contrast, there were heavy concentrations of unemployment in construction, the distributive trades and miscellaneous services, accounting for 14.5, 9.7 and 10.2 per cent respectively of total unemployment. However, since the geographic incidence of these activities is fairly widely spread throughout the country they have not given rise to the same extreme regional variations in unemployment as was the case with the staple industries in the inter-war years.

A further notable feature of the current situation is the sheltered nature of the public sector. In May 1982, when total unemployment was approaching 3 million, a mere 255,000 were registered as unemployed in the public sector, equivalent to 3.4 per cent of total public sector employment (7½ million).[7] The burden of unemployment is therefore very much a private sector one, whereas the enormous growth in public employment through to the 1970s, and the sheltered nature of most of the occupations in this sector, meant that for the most part the public sector has emerged unscathed from the recent labour shake-out elsewhere in the economy. There are no parallels in this respect with the earlier period since public sector employment was then still very small. How far the recent rapid growth in public sector employment has been responsible for the squeeze in manufacturing employment and the private sector as a whole is a matter of contentious debate, but overall it has probably done little to improve the latter's prospects.

TABLE 1.5: **Regional Unemployment Rates 1965-82 (quarter 4)**[1]

Region	1965	1973	1979	1982[2]
East Anglia	1.2	1.6	4.1	10.2
South-east	0.8	1.3	3.4	9.2
South-west	1.5	2.1	5.2	10.7
West Midlands	0.6	1.7	5.2	15.0
East Midlands	0.9	1.8	4.4	11.0
Yorkshire and Humberside	1.0	2.3	5.2	13.0
North	2.3	3.9	8.0	16.1
North-west	1.4	2.9	6.6	15.1
Wales	2.5	3.0	7.1	15.7
Scotland	2.7	3.8	7.5	14.4
Great Britain	1.3	2.2	5.2	12.3

Notes: 1. Numbers unemployed excluding school-leavers expressed as a percentage of the latest available mid-year estimates of all employees in employment plus unemployed at the same date.
2. Quarter 3.

Source: Central Statistical Office, *Economic Trends: Annual Supplement* (1983 Edition), pp. 106-9.

TABLE 1.6: **Regional Unemployment Rates 1912/13 – 1929/36 (July each year)**[1]

Region	1912-13	1929	1932	Average 1929-36
London	8.7	4.7	13.1	8.8
South-east	4.7	3.8	13.1	7.8
South-west	4.6	6.8	16.4	11.1
Midlands	3.1/2.5[2]	9.5	21.6	15.2
North-east	2.5	12.6	30.6	22.7
North-west	2.7	12.7	26.3	21.6
Scotland	1.8	11.2	29.0	21.8
Wales	3.1	18.8	38.1	30.1
Great Britain	3.9	9.7	22.9	16.9
South Britain	—	6.4	16.2	11.0
North Britain and Wales	—	12.9	29.5	22.8

Notes: 1. For the pre-war period the figures refer only to unemployment in trade unions, while the Ministry of Labour's data for the inter-war period covers only insured workers and does not include unemployed workers who failed to register at the employment exchanges.

2. West and East Midlands respectively.

Source: D. H. Aldcroft, *The Interwar Economy: Britain 1919-1939* (1970), p. 80.

The contrasting regional incidence of unemployment is borne out by the regional unemployment data for the two periods. It should be stressed that the statistical data for the current period are much more comprehensive than that for the earlier period since the inter-war unemployment returns only covered insured workers where the incidence of unemployment was higher than elsewhere. Hence the regional unemployment rates for this period are higher than the standardised aggregate rates for the whole labour force given in Table 1.1, as they do not include data for that part of the workforce excluded from the national insurance scheme. However, they may be used to draw broad comparisons with the current period.

Regional unemployment rates for selected years in the two periods are given in Tables 1.5 and 1.6. What is most noticeable is the much stronger regional incidence of unemployment in the inter-war years. The most prosperous regions of the country, London and the south-east, had an unemployment rate of about one-half the average for Great Britain in most years, whereas in the worst affected regions of the North (including Wales) unemployment was two to three times greater than in the south-east. A similar discrepancy existed prior to 1914, but then the ranking was reversed with the northern regions recording very much much lower unemployment rates than those in the south of the country. At the county and local levels there were some very sharp differences indeed during the inter-war period. For example, at the peak of recovery in 1937 Middlesex, Bedfordshire and Buckinghamshire had insured unemployment rates of only 4.8 per cent, whereas in Anglesey, Brecknock, Banff and Caithness and Sutherland they still averaged around one-third. Equally notable were the very marked local differences within the same county: Chelmsford in the prosperous county of Essex had a rate as low as 1.6 per cent in 1937 as against 36.4 per cent at Pitsea: while in Glamorgan, the rate at Resolven was 4.5 per cent but that at Ferndale was no less than 48.1 per cent.[8]

Regional contrasts persisted throughout the post-war period, though they appeared less glaring in the full employment era of the 1950s and 1960s, and in more recent years there has been some narrowing of regional differentials. It is true that in the mid-1960s Scotland, Wales and the North of England had unemployment rates which were double or treble those of the more prosperous regions of the West Midlands, East Midlands, Yorkshire, East Anglia and the south-east, but during the 1970s, when unemployment rates rose sharply throughout the country, the great regional and local disparities of the 1930s were considerably reduced. Currently (third quarter of 1982) the West Midlands and the north-west, once regions of low unemployment, are now the worst affected in the country, along with Scotland, Wales and the North. At the same time, unemployment levels in the South have risen rapidly in the last few years so that the differences between the best and the worst regions have been reduced to 75 per cent or less as against 200 – 300 per cent in the first two post-war decades. Currently, the four worst affected regions, the North, north-west, the West Midlands and Wales have rates of unemployment some 22 – 30 percent above the average for Great Britain as a whole, and over 50 per cent higher than the level in the most favoured region of the south-east. By contrast, in the 1930s the northern regions and Wales had rates of unemployment two to three times those in the south-east of England. Furthermore, throughout the period 1929 – 36 unemployment in the north-east, north-west, Scotland and Wales exceeded the national average by 34, 28, 29 and 78 per cent respectively, whereas in the latter part of 1982 the five regions with the heaviest unemployment exceeded the average for the whole country by 31 per cent or less: the North 31 per cent, Wales 28 per cent, the north-west 23 per cent, the West Midlands 22 per cent and Scotland 17 per cent.

Thus while regional disparities continue to exist the differences are noticeably less than those recorded in the 1930s, and even the former great North – South differential is becoming somewhat blurred as unemployment mounts rapidly in the once prosperous regions like the West Midlands, and to a lesser extent in the south-east. The narrowing of the regional differentials is not altogether surprising given the more widespread dispersion of unemployment among industries and other sectors of the economy, many of which are far less spatially concentrated than was the case in the inter-war period. Structural imbalances within the regions still remain of course, and there are some localities with very high rates of unemployment, but in the wider regional context the differences have narrowed as a result of the contraction of the old basic industries which accounted for a large share of employment in the northern regions, and because of the steady adaptation of the economic structure of the northern regions to the changes in the patterns of demand of the post-war period.

Prior to 1939 the chief problem of the northern regions and Wales was their very heavy dependence on a small group of staple industries, the markets for whose products virtually collapsed largely, though not entirely, as a result of the severe deterioration in the export trade. More specifically, in almost every year between 45-50 per cent of total unemployment was to be found in five areas (south-west, Scotland, the north-east coast, Lancashire/ Merseyside and South Wales) which collectively accounted for less than one-third of the insured population and just over one-quarter of the total population of the country.[9] Rates of unemployment in these regions were twice or more the national average and for most of the time they were losing employment. The main difficulty lay in the excessive reliance on a narrow industrial basis – mining, mechanical engineering, metal manufacture, textiles, and shipbuilding – industries whose markets were collapsing and which, as we have seen were responsible for a large share of total unemployment.

Given the strong localisation of the staple industries in the North, it is easy to see why this part of the country suffered so much more than the South. Scotland, for example, was particularly vulnerable from the point of view of industrial structure. The old staple industries accounted for 43.2 and 36.8 per cent of Scotland's net industrial output in 1924 and 1935 respectively, as against 37 and 27.8 per cent respectively for the UK as a whole: conversely, the share of the new growth industries (vehicles, electrical engineering, rayon, non-ferrous metals, paper, printing and publishing) in Scotland's net industrial output was 8.3 and 11.0 per cent in the years in question compared with national percentages of 14.1 and 21 per cent. Scotland's problem stemmed primarily from the dramatic collapse of export demand for her once staple products. The volume of exports through Scottish ports fell by no less than 56 per cent between 1913 and 1933, and even at the peak of recovery in 1937 they were still 42 per cent below the pre-war level. Moreover, the heavy dependence on declining basic sectors resulted in lower productivity and lower income per head than in Great Britain as a whole, and this in turn tended to discourage the development of new and expanding sectors of activity.

A similar story could be recounted for the other northern regions and for Wales, where in some localities the old staple industries accounted for some 60 – 70 per cent of the insured labour force. By contrast, in the South of the country and parts of the Midlands, with their more favourable locational advantages in terms of markets and incomes, together with more flexible and diverse economic structures, the pressure was eased by the rapid growth of newer industries, building (especially residential construction) and the service trades, though even here the growth of employment was insufficient to cope with both local unemployment and the drift of workers from the North. Moreover, the problem was compounded during the period, as it is today though partly for different reasons, by a general rise in productive efficiency due to technical change and cost pressures, and also by the fact that some of the newer sectors of activity were more capital-intensive than the older branches of industry. The overall impact of these changes was to reduce the input of labour per unit of output. Even in some of the old staple industries, such as cotton and coal, improved efficiency and technical change were having a marked effect on the demand for labour.[10]

If regional differences in unemployment are less evident today than in the 1930s, there is some evidence to suggest that occupational and age differentials are now somewhat more pronounced than in the past. Bosanquet, for example, notes that differences between groups of workers are as important as differences between places, and that a person's prospects in the labour market now depend almost as much upon his occupational status and his age as on the area or locality in which he lives.[11] Increasing unemployment has of course always tended to fall with greater incidence upon the less skilled workers, especially manual workers, since they are the easiest to dispense with when economic conditions deteriorate. However, it seems that in the last decade or so their relative position in the labour market has deteriorated since unemployment among semi-skilled and manual workers has risen more rapidly than unemployment as a whole, whereas this was not generally the case in the 1930s. Nor was youth unemployment so pronounced in that decade as it is today. It is true that juvenile unemployment (under 18 years of age) rose sharply between 1929 and 1932 from over 3 per cent among boys in 1929 to 8.3 per cent in 1932,[12] but even at the latter date it was still only just over one-third of the national adult average rate; thereafter it rose steeply and reached the general average between the ages of 21 – 24. By contrast, youth unemployment

16

today is higher than for any other age group at nearly twice the rate for all workers and nearly three times the rate prevailing among workers in the 35 – 54 age band. Thereafter the incidence of unemployment increases as workers approach retirement age and the differential narrows. Among older workers (60+) unemployment is above the average for all age groups.

While there is a noticeable contrast in the age distribution of unemployment between the two periods, the same cannot be said for its duration, which tends to follow a similar pattern. Generally speaking, the longer high unemployment persists the greater becomes the volume of long-term unemployment, particularly among older workers who find increasing difficulty, on account of age, skills, health and other factors, to secure renewed permanent employment. Thus in 1936 and 1937 some one-quarter of the applicants for unemployment benefit had been out of work for a year or more compared with less than 5 per cent in 1929.[13] Though the actual risk of losing one's job was much the same at all ages from 35 to 64, once having lost a job the older person found it much more difficult to regain employment and was therefore likely to swell the ranks of the long-term unemployed. As Beveridge noted,

The older man has less power of recovery industrially from loss of employment, as he has less power of recovery physically, from sickness or accident. Once he has become unemployed, he is more likely than a younger man to remain unemployed; and he is much more likely to become chronically unemployed. Prolonged unemployment falls with crushing weight on the older men, once they have lost their niche in industry. The risk of losing one's job is much the same from 60 to 64 as it is from 35 to 44. The risk of being out of a job is half as much again at the later age than at the earlier age; the risk of becoming chronically unemployed, that is to say of being out for more than a year, is $2\frac{1}{2}$ times as great.[14]

The uneven distribution of long-period unemployment among the regions confirms the view that it was the older workers in the older regions and industries who were likely to suffer the brunt of prolonged unemployment. In June 1937 less than 10 per cent of the unemployment applicants in London and the south-east had been unemployed for 12 months or more, while 67 – 71 per cent had been out for less than 3 months. By contrast, 33 – 40 per cent of the applicants in the North, Scotland and Wales had been on benefit for a year or more, whereas short-period unemployment (under 3 months) accounted for less than 40 per cent. In the South of Britain (London, the south-east, the south-west and the Midlands) long-period unemployment accounted for 12½ per cent of the unemployment as against nearly 30 per cent in North Britain and Wales, while the corresponding figures for short-period unemployment were 66.7 and 48.0 per cent respectively.[15]

Long-period unemployment in the early 1980s is of a similar order of magnitude, and again its age distribution is very skewed tending to fall most heavily on workers over 55, and least on those below 25, a difference which may have become more pronounced in recent years owing to the greater emphasis on youth employment policies compared with the 1930s. Thus in January 1982 of the unemployed workers aged 55 and over 44 per cent had been unemployed for more than a year as against only 17 per cent in the case of those under 25; conversely, in the latter category, unemployment was primarily of relatively short duration (up to 26 weeks) accounting for 61 per cent of younger workers as against only 34 per cent for older workers.[16]

Finally a note should be made of the distribution of unemployment by sex. In this regard precise specification and comparison is difficult since here data collection presents special problems. For various reasons, some of which reflect the provisions of the different national insurance schemes, women are less likely to register as unemployed than men. This was particularly true of the 1930s when women were discriminated against and female employment predominated in occupations such as domestic service and teaching which were excluded from the national insurance schemes. On the other hand, due to the rapid rise in the women's employment participation ratio in the post-war period, women now account for 40 per cent or more of the labour force, about double the share in the 1930s. This would tend to increase their exposure to unemployment, partly offset by the fact that a large share of the total comprised older and/or married women and part-time workers who have a low registration rate because of the restricted nature of the benefits under the insurance schemes. In other words, the true unemployment rate among female workers will tend to be understated in the official returns. For what they are worth, the figures show that unemployment among young females (under 19) is high and almost matches that of males of the same age; thereafter it falls sharply to less than half the male rate from the age of 35 onwards. The current average rate for all age groups is over half the male rate. The ratios between female and male unemployment were lower, though not markedly so, before the war; in November 1932, for example, the average insured unemployment rate for males was 21.8 and that for females 9.5 per cent. This is more or less what one might expect given the limited incentive to register and the lower exposure of females to cyclically-prone activities. What the true rates would be if all unemployed women had registered is anybody's guess, though one might still expect the unemployment rate to be lower among women than among males, given the latter's greater exposure to unemployment-prone industrial activities.[17]

In conclusion, despite some marked differences in the characteristics of unemployment between the 1930s and the present, it is a fact that the distribution of unemployment remains very uneven between trades, occupations and regions. The burden of unemployment falls very heavily on particular categories of workers. The young, the old and the unskilled tend to suffer most severely, both in terms of duration of unemployment and the frequency of its occurrence. Moreover, only a minority of the population are likely to experience such hardship. It has been estimated that something like 70 per cent of all weeks of unemployment in a single year are borne by only 3 per cent of the working population, whereas if unemployment were equally distributed throughout the labour force, in that no one individual experienced more than one spell of unemployment in a year, some 17 per cent of the working population would be affected, rising to 50 per cent over a three-year period.[18] Whether such characteristics reflect in part the structural nature of unemployment is a point to which we shall return in later chapters.

NOTES

1 See A. Maddison, *Economic Policy and Performance in Europe, 1913-1970* (1973), p. 15.
2 See W. R. Garside, *The Measurement of Unemployment in Great Britain, 1850-1979* (1980), for a discussion of the problems in interpreting the unemployment statistics.
3 A. P. Thirlwall, 'Deindustrialisation in the United Kingdom', *Lloyds Bank Review*, **144** (April 1982), pp. 26-7.
4 See *Financial Times*, 9 December 1982.
5 M. Semple, 'Employment in the Public and Private Sectors, 1961-78', *Economic Trends*, **313** (November 1979), pp. 90-108.
6 See Lord Snowden, *Mr. Lloyd George's New Deal* (1935), p. 6.
7 W. A. P. Manser, 'Cut Public Over-employment', *Journal of Economic Affairs*, 3 (October 1982), pp. 54-5.
8 See M. P. Fogarty, *Prospects of the Industrial Areas of Great Britain* (1945), Table 8, pp. 18-19; and W. H. Beveridge, *Full Employment in a Free Society* (1944), pp. 324-7.
9 E. D. McCullum, 'The Problem of the Depressed Areas in Great Britain', *International Labour Review*, 30 (August 1934), p. 137.
10 G. M. Beck, *A Survey of British Employment and Unemployment, 1927-45* (1951), pp. 16-17.
11 N. Bosanquet, 'Structuralism and Structural Unemployment', *British Journal of Industrial Relations*, **17** (1979), p. 310.
12 W. R. Garside, 'Juvenile Unemployment and Public Policy between the Wars', *Economic History Review*, **30** (1977).
13 K. Hawkins, *Unemployment* (1979), p. 21.
14 Beveridge, *op. cit.*, pp. 70-1.
15 Ibid., pp. 67-8; Royal Institute for International Affairs, *Unemployment: An International Problem* (1935), pp. 55-7.
16 J. Tomlinson, 'Unemployment and Policy in the 1930s and 1980s', *Three Banks Review*, **135** (September 1982), p. 21.
17 Though a higher turnover rate among females may offset this to some extent.
18 J. Creedy (ed.), *The Economics of Unemployment in Britain* (1981), p. 171.

2 Unemployment and Economic Policy

From an economic point of view there are striking similarities between the 1930s and the 1980s, as well as some notable contrasts. This chapter presents a review of the economic background to the unemployment problem in the two periods, together with the policy reactions of the respective governments. In the final section a brief comment is made on the alternative strategies to those adopted. Except in so far as it is relevant to the analysis which follows in later chapters, the causes of unemployment are not examined in detail since the main purpose of the present volume is to discuss the constraints to a full employment policy.

ECONOMIC BACKGROUND

That the heavy unemployment of the 1930s and 1980s is in part a product of depression few would deny, though it should be noted that both periods were preceded by a long-term deterioration in employment opportunities. Comparative data for the changes in key economic variables during the three major depressions of the twentieth century are given in Table 2.1, and these provide a good indication of the extent to which activity declined. The figures suggest that in many respects the current recession is as severe, if not more so, than that of 1929 – 32, but not quite as bad as that following the first world war. The worst hit sector in the current recession has been manufacturing, with a decline of 18 per cent over the last three years, which means that manufacturing output is now lower than it was in the early 1970s. Industrial production has held up rather better because of the rising output of oil and gas, though even here the decline in the last three years has been greater than 1929 – 32. Only in the slump after the first world war did industrial production and total output fall more sharply.

TABLE 2.1: **Percentage Change in Selected Economic Indicators during Three Downswings**

	1920-1	*1929-32*	*1979(2)-1982(2)*
Gross domestic product	-12.2	-4.8	-6.7
Manufacturing production	-22.2	-10.3	-18.0
Industrial production	-18.6	-10.8	-12.7
Exports (volume)	-30.1	-37.5	0.0
Employment	-14.4	-4.7	-8.9
Retail prices	-9.2	-12.2	48.4
Wholesale prices	-35.8	-25.6	47.0

Sources: C. H. Feinstein, *National Income, Expenditure and Output of the United Kingdom, 1855-1965* (1972); D. H. Aldcroft, *The Interwar Economy: Britain 1919-1939* (1970), p.34; *Economic Trends.*

One notable difference between the two periods is in the movement of exports. Despite the severity of the current recession, and the strength of sterling through to 1981 due to pressures in the oil market, exports have remained surprisingly resilient; disregarding short-term fluctuations, there has been little change in the total volume of exports since the middle of 1979. This is in sharp contrast to the inter-war period when in both recessions exports fell by 30 per cent or more. One should of course bear in mind that world trade fell very sharply in the 1930s and that Britain was particularly exposed in this respect given the high proportion of exports coming from the ex-growth staple industries such as coal, shipbuilding and textiles. More recently, world trade has at worst been stagnant while Britain's external trade has been bolstered by the rising volume of oil exports.

Perhaps the greatest contrast between the two periods is the trend in prices. For most of the inter-war period prices were drifting downwards, and in the depressions of 1920-1 and 1929-32 they fell very steeply indeed being influenced strongly by the downward trend in commodity prices as a result of over-supply problems in many products. By contrast, as can be seen from Table 2.1, prices during the last three years have risen by nearly 50 per cent despite the recession and the flatness of commodity prices in the latter half of the period, though there has been a considerable moderation in the rate of inflation over the period as a whole. These inflationary conditions have had important implications for policy as we shall see in Chapter 6.

Though Britain suffered severe unemployment and a sharp decline in exports during 1929-32, the macro-economic indicators suggest that in terms of income and total output the recession was less severe than in many of the major industrial countries. Germany, France, Austria, Belgium and the United States, for example, all experienced much steeper declines in gross domestic product and industrial production than did Britain.[1] Conversely, the more recent period has seen a deterioration in Britain's relative economic performance *vis-à-vis* her major competitors, in terms of output, employment and inflation. In fact, through to 1981 most industrial countries recorded expansion in output and employment, albeit very modest, while unemployment rates, though rising, were still well below those of the UK. Until recently, the UK's inflation record has been poorer than average. Only in one respect, that of productivity, has Britain performed better than her rivals, and then mainly due to the enormous shake-out of labour, especially from the manufacturing sector. However, the trend rate of productivity growth has only been marginally better than in the past, while in terms of competitiveness it was offset by the sharp rise in the exchange rate between 1978 and the first quarter of 1981. Despite a fall since then in the exchange rate, Britain's competitiveness in early 1982 was estimated to have deteriorated by some 35 per cent compared with 1978, though there has been some improvement in the last year or so due to the continued decline in the sterling exchange rate.[2]

Given the severity of the depressions in the 1930s and 1980s, it is scarcely surprising that unemployment soared upwards. But one cannot attribute all the unemployment to cyclical

23

factors, and it is important therefore in the context of later analysis to look at the longer-term economic background to unemployment, to determine how far it was caused by structural factors, in which secular changes in patterns of demand, technology, etc. give rise to permanent shifts in the pattern of resource requirements in particular sectors thereby producing a state of persistent unemployment in those sectors. Such structural problems may not be confined to specific sectors of the economy. Structural adjustment may be required over a fairly wide spectrum of the economy when accumulated competitive losses and inflation create the need for adjustment (see Chapter 6).

Both periods were preceded by a decade or so of chequered and disturbed development prior to which there had been sustained growth. The pattern is not identical in every respect, but the similarities are worth stressing, and in particular the transformation problems created by structural tensions between ex-growth industries and the new and/or potential growth industries.

Before 1914 the major industrial powers enjoyed a period of almost uninterrupted and harmonious growth (that is, in the sense of no serious disparities in performance and costs and prices) based on the application of proven technologies and exploitation of cheap energy sources, though with some flagging in investment opportunities prior to the war as developments in new fields were slow to mature. This is particularly true of Britain, where heavy concentration of resources in a few major staple industries and weak development in new lines of activity were partly responsible for her less satisfactory performance compared with her major competitors.

The war and its aftermath dealt a severe shock to the economic system. Apart from the financial problems to which it gave rise, it distorted economic relationships and produced a hiatus in investment opportunities as staple industries based on old technologies lost their growth momentum while new technologies were still in the stage of infancy. The results were excess capacity and structural problems some of which were undoubtedly intensified by the legacies of the war, and during the 1920s many countries experienced rather erratic patterns of development, not unlike those of the 1970s. The United

States was something of an exception in this respect. Having emerged from the war in a very strong position, with an industrial base already better adapted to the future, the United States enjoyed a strong boom in the 1920s based on residential construction and the first major phase of the application of new technologies in motor transport, electrical development, and the like. Unfortunately, the boom overshot itself, markets became temporarily saturated and the economy slid into recession in 1929, dragging the rest of the world with it. It is perhaps significant that the recovery of the American economy in the 1930s was decidedly weak.

The British case provides a marked contrast to the American. Before 1914 and through the 1920s Britain was lagging behind her major competitors. She was slow to exploit new investment opportunities in growth potential sectors and she had too large a volume of resources locked up in the ex-growth staple industries (coal, textiles and shipbuilding in particular), which in themselves were overmanned and inefficient. Thus, after the war, when markets for export-orientated industries collapsed due to shifting demand patterns and changes in technology, there was little to fill the gap. Hence the heavy unemployment and severe structural problems of the older regions and industries in the first post-war decade and the rather muted nature of the upswing in the later 1920s. On the other hand, structural transformation was taking place slowly, and the initial lag in the development of new technologies, or more strictly in their application, meant that, unlike the United States, real growth forces were strong in Britain in the 1930s. Hence the sustained recovery from the slump of 1932 based on residential construction and new technologies.

A rather similar scenario can be written for the post-war period. After the reconstruction phase of the late 1940s, which was quicker and more effective than after the first world war due to the absence of major policy blunders, all the major industrial countries experienced a lengthy period of expansion with rates of growth far surpassing anything recorded previously. Britain shared in the boom though her progress was more sedate. This sustained expansion was based on the massive exploitation of energy-intensive sectors of activity and new technologies (especially in consumer durables) and was assisted by relatively low fuel prices and a moderate improvement in the terms of trade between industrial and primary producing countries. It eventually culminated in the hectic boom of 1972-3, which was accompanied by big increases in commodity and energy prices thereby aggravating the inflationary pressures already apparent from the late 1960s. After 1973, growth was much more erratic and protracted; there was a sharp downturn in 1974-5, a modest revival through to the later 1970s, after which stagnation set in through to the present. As in the 1920s, Britain's performance showed relative weakness, this time not so much through over-commitment to a narrow range of industries but rather to an economy-wide loss of competitive strength.

The disturbed economic and financial conditions of the 1970s were similar to those of the 1920s, but these should not obscure the fact that in both cases the underlying growth forces were weakening after a period of prolonged expansion. This is particularly the case in the more recent period given the massive boom and rapid exploitation of new technologies, and it is not therefore surprising that there should be some exhaustion of investment opportunities subsequently. In other words, western development was likely to experience some slowing-down in the pace of development after the early 1970s irrespective of the shocks imparted during that turbulent decade which undoubtedly contributed to the slowing-down of expansion in both old and new fields of endeavour. Again, as in the earlier period, the exhaustion of technological opportunities gave rise to structural problems, notably excess capacity in older sectors such as steel, heavy chemicals, petrochemicals and mechanical engineering, with developments in growth potential industries – electronics, nuclear power, new consumer durables, pharmaceuticals, information research – taking time to mature.

It is important to stress these longer-term structural transformation problems, involving as they do a shift of resources from older sectors of activity with very limited growth potential to newer, higher technology sectors with strong future growth prospects. There is often a hiatus between technological transformations of this type, that is until what have been termed the 'sunrise industries' can take the place of the decaying sectors.[3] In the meantime the economic system will suffer from excess capacity and higher unemployment than normally warranted by cyclical factors. Britain, moreover, has a persistent and more pervasive structural problem as a result of competitive losses and inflationary pressures.

The main difficulty is that of determining the extent of non-cyclical or structural unemployment. One of the main problems of course is defining exactly what is meant by structural unemployment. Turvey, for example, sees it in terms of a mismatch between unemployed and job vacancies such that if the former were retrained and/or relocated, the level of unemployment would fall, a process which would be unlikely to occur in a poor labour market.[4] This is however a rather narrow and restrictive definition, the results of which clearly depend upon the state of cyclical unemployment. Moreover, it does not take into account the potential unemployment in those sectors experiencing secular decline whose employment prospects may be artificially and temporarily boosted in times of buoyant activity and full employment. Hence it is not surprising that Turvey finds relatively little structural unemployment through to the mid-1970s despite the fact that over one-fifth of industrial employment was located in declining sectors of the economy.

Structural unemployment has certainly increased since 1975. Indeed, if we define it in terms of persistent unemployment in sectors where secular forces (shifts in competitive strength, changes in demand patterns, market imperfections, technologies and productivity) give rise to long-term contraction in employment opportunities, irrespective of the opportunities which may or may not be available elsewhere in the economy, then there can be little doubt that it has risen sharply in many branches of activity where long-term growth prospects are very limited, for example, mechanical engineering, heavy chemicals, petro-chemicals, steel, textiles and shipbuilding.[5] Former employment levels in these sectors will never be regained simply because there is no longer the same demand for their products as in the past. In such cases therefore one-half or more of their registered unemployment may be due to long-term structural problems rather than demand deficiency of a cyclical nature.

Precise estimates of the amount of structural unemployment are difficult to derive though a number of tentative calculations have been made for the inter-war years. Keynes, for example, believed that not all unemployment was receptive to demand management; there was a residue of what he called 'normal' unemployment which he put at 800,000 for the inter-war years, though only a quarter of this total was due to misfits of trade and locality. However, more than half the 'abnormal' unemployment he regarded as being due to a transfer problem some of which could be attributed to structural factors.[6] Beveridge, on the other hand, defined persistent unemployment as those out of work for 9 months or more, and on this basis he produced a figure of 500,000 for July 1936.[7] Fogarty used London and the south-east as a yardstick by which to measure the general level of unemployment in each region. Unemployment in any region over and above this norm or general level could be termed excess unemployment, providing a measure of prosperity for each region. On this basis he found that general unemployment for Britain as a whole in 1932 worked out at nearly 1.7 million, as against an actual unemployment total of over 2.7 million, thus giving a total excess unemployment of about 1 million. In the cyclical peak years of 1929 and 1937 excess unemployment for Britain as a whole amounted to between 570 – 580,000 out of a total unemployment of 1.2 and 1.4 million respectively; practically all of this could be classed as persistent excess unemployment caused by structural factors.[8]

These calculations may however understate the degree of structural unemployment in this period, especially in the latter part of the period. By 1937, following a sharp upswing, most of the cyclical unemployment had been eliminated yet total unemployment in that year was still above the previous cyclical peak even though domestic output and industrial production had increased considerably during the intervening period (1929 – 37). In other words, because of shifts in the production structure, due to changes in demand patterns, technology and improvements in efficiency, the economy was producing considerably more than in 1929 with lower labour inputs. It is this kind of transformation which produces the structural unemployment and the latter type of unemployment becomes more pronounced during a deep and prolonged recession since it induces the search for better and more economical methods of production which reduce the demand for labour. The same process has been taking place in the 1970s and early 1980s with the added pressure from inflation and labour market rigidities which have stimulated the need to make labour-saving economies, for which there is considerable scope given the low level of efficiency of British industry. Such factors tend to drive up the long-term natural rate of unemployment (see Chapter 6). We shall return to these issues in later chapters. For the moment it would seem not implausible to suggest that perhaps around one-half the unemployment of the late 1930s (some 750,000) was of a structural kind.[9] A conservative estimate for structural unemployment today would be about one-third, that is 1 million persons.

While it may be difficult to specify precisely the structural content of unemployment, it is important to emphasise the fact that it is by no means negligible. Moreover, the longer a period of high unemployment persists, the more likely it is that the volume of structural unemployment will increase as workers and capacity in older branches of industry become redundant and obsolete with the passage of time. This raises important issues with respect to the type of policy required to deal with this kind of unemployment.

POLICY REACTIONS TO UNEMPLOYMENT

The reactions of policy-makers to recession and unemployment were similar in both periods. Macro-economic policy (fiscal and monetary) was tightened considerably. This is particularly true on the fiscal side since attempts were made to balance the budget or reduce budgetary deficits which entailed a squeeze on public spending. Thus, in terms of a constant employment balance, the budgetary stance became progressively more restrictive. For the most part monetary policy was designed to complement the fiscal stance (or vice versa) so that the net effect was that macro-policy became a source of income destruction rather than one of income creation. Secondly, specific measures were taken to alleviate the more severe fall-

ffects of the depression, for example, defensive measures
op up ailing sectors of the economy as with the industrial
reconstruction schemes of the 1930s or the subsidies to 'lame
duck' industries in the 1970s and 1980s; similarly there were
schemes for regional assistance, industrial transfer and new
training opportunities.

Some contrasts in the policy approach are worth noting. In
the more recent period much greater emphasis has been placed
on removing barriers and controls on enterprise and markets,
whereas during the 1930s the trend was towards a greater
degree of restriction on competition. On the other hand, in the
1930s three policies were implemented which do not have exact
counterparts in the 1980s. First, the currency was formally
devalued in September 1931 when Britain left the gold
standard; for a time Britain gained a competitive advantage
until most other countries followed suit, with the result that by
the middle of the decade the effective exchange rate was more
or less back to the 1929 level.[10] Secondly, tariffs and import
restrictions were widely adopted from 1932 onwards, together
with Imperial preference, though their role in recovery is still a
matter of controversy. Thirdly, monetary policy was relaxed in
1932, at least in so far as interest rates were concerned, though
monetary growth continued to be constrained by the fiscal
stance. The real rate of interest was still positive, though the
margin was less than it is today.

While ideological factors played an important part in
determining the specific policy response in both cases, the
policy packages did have an underlying motive, namely that of
creating favourable conditions for a spontaneous economic
recovery; since this in turn depended upon the competitiveness
of the economy it was felt that it would be facilitated by a
lowering of the real wage level (see Chapter 6). Employment
creation was not a specific objective of policy but a residual
one since the political and economic ideology of governments
in the 1930s and 1980s precluded a radical programme of
action designed to generate employment.

The ideological constraints to radical policies have been
discussed on numerous occasions and can therefore be dealt
with briefly here. In the 1930s classical economic precepts still
held sway, which in practical terms meant that budgets should

be balanced, government spending contained and deficit financing avoided at all costs. Hence the restrictive budgetary out-turn of the period. The current ideology of 'Thatchernomics' is not dissimilar since it involves restraints on public spending and the reduction of budgetary deficits, control of the money supply and maintenance of the exchange rate. Again, a radical programme of work creation would not be contemplated under the present administration, since the whole *raison d'être* of government policy is to create the conditions for a spontaneous recovery, which in practical terms depends in part on defeating inflation. However, irrespective of the political and economic thought of the day we believe that there are in fact powerful financial and economic constraints which render full employment an elusive goal.

It would be futile to deny that the policies adopted were anything but harmful to output and employment. It has long since been accepted that restrictive policy action will tend to exacerbate any downturn in economic activity. Pratten, for example, has demonstrated the influence of Mrs Thatcher's economic policies, though it is important to note that possibly less than half the underlying increase in unemployment since July 1979 can be accounted for by government macro-intervention in the economy compared with a mild Keynesian alternative.[11] Similarly, it would be difficult to maintain that all the unemployment of the 1930s was caused by economic policy. The fact is that in both periods there was a longer-term deterioration in employment opportunities beyond the range of specific government action.

It is not the purpose of the present exercise, however, to refute the logic of the facts. Rather it is to question the feasibility of finding a quick and viable solution to large-scale unemployment, part of the very nature of which defies a ready solution in conventional terms. Apart from the structural aspects of the problem – the longer-term implications of which are explored in Chapter 4 – the very magnitude of the task makes it difficult to engineer a speedy solution without coming up against economic and financial constraints. While these are not always readily appreciated in the policy prescriptions frequently advanced, there has at least been a reluctant

31

admission on the part of many commentators that a state of full employment will take many years to achieve. Indeed few, if any, of the proposals currently in vogue envisage an easy and rapid return to full employment. One of the more pessimistic over the medium term is the University of Warwick's Manpower Research Group. In the Group's *Review* of early 1981, the authors outlined a programme to create over ½ million jobs by the middle of the decade, but they went on to warn that

no policy package, including that of the present administration, is now capable of reducing registered unemployment much below 2½ million by 1985. Over the rest of the decade the only way in which unemployment could be reduced substantially – say to the 1½ million with which the decade began – would be through the introduction of severe import controls [which] we are not prepared to advocate.[12]

Though generally more optimistic on the scope for policy action, the TUC and the Labour Party confess that even their large spending proposals and other policy measures, including a substantial devaluation of sterling, will not produce a dramatic decline in the unemployment total, while the policy measures would take several years to complete. Thus the TUC's five-year £24 billion programme of public investment, outlined in *The Reconstruction of Industry* in August 1981, was estimated to generate some ½ million jobs by 1986, and even this was probably a rather optimistic projection.[13] In fact, what is remarkable about most of the current proposed remedies is their modest nature, involving at best the creation of some ½ million jobs over a period of years.[14] Indeed, some proposed policy packages set their targets even lower, notably that of Hopkin, Miller and Reddaway, which realises a reduction in recorded unemployment of only 320,000.[15] And even the more radical proposals, involving large devaluations and import controls, fail to bring the projected unemployment totals down to respectable levels (below 2 million) over the decade.[16] At this point one might recall the equally modest spending plans of Lloyd George half a century earlier, which it was tentatively hoped would produce new jobs of a similar order of magnitude (see Chapter 3). Even the radicals, it seems, retreat in the face of adversity!

POLICY OPTIONS AND ASSUMPTIONS

Given the rather modest nature of many of the current policy proposals – at least in terms of the employment impact – it might be asked whether there is much to be lost in waiting for spontaneous recovery. This basically was the option that was adopted in the 1930s – with a little help from policy via cheap money – and as it turned out there was a strong cyclical upswing through to 1937 with unemployment falling by roughly one-half from the trough of 1931 – 2. This still of course left some 1½ million out of work by the end of the decade. There is little doubt that spontaneous recovery will develop in the course of the 1980s, but both the timing and the strength of any recovery remain in question to date. Most commentators believe that it will be relatively weak when it comes, and that it will be barely sufficient to accommodate the increase in working population, let alone make any indentation on the 3 million or so currently on the unemployment register. Under these circumstances, a strong case could be made for formulating a bold programme of action designed to restore full employment during the course of the decade. The question therefore remains to test the feasibility of such a policy under various constraints.

The assumptions and policy options are as follows. We take as the central objective that of creating some 3 million jobs in the early 1930s and 1980s. This is a realistic target for the current period given the probable increase in the working population, but it may be a little on the high side for the 1930s. The policy action is assumed to start at the trough of the depression, say around 1932 and hopefully 1982, and it is further assumed that Britain takes unilateral action which means that all the major countries do not deviate significantly from their prevailing policy stance. The next task is to designate the policy options. The range of possible policy measures is somewhat greater today than it was in the 1930s including some such as incomes policies and changes in the National Insurance Surcharge which have no relevance to the earlier period. On the other hand, as noted earlier, in the 1930s some policy instruments such as tariffs, import controls and

33

cheap money were pressed into service which today are still on the drawing board. While each of these policies may contribute to employment generation, their individual contribution is sometimes small and rather indirect, while monetary policy may be regarded more as a permissive and indirect instrument designed to encourage spontaneous recovery. The two most important are probably import controls and incomes policies, but both raise special problems as regards implementation, and in any case they have been advocated more as an adjunct to a general policy of reflation in order to deal with the problems arising from the latter policy.

The two most widely canvassed policy alternatives have been fiscal reflation and devaluation, and it is on these that we shall concentrate in the first instance. Both are highly relevant to the two periods in question thereby facilitating a comparative approach. What might now be regarded as a conventional instrument, namely fiscal reflation, was favoured in certain quarters in the inter-war years and of course it has been advocated time and again today. Likewise, devaluation has many supporters given the alleged over-valuation of sterling, though in a sense it is simply a logical (inevitable?) outcome of a policy of reflation. While at first glance depreciation of the currency might seem irrelevant in the context of the 1930s, given the devaluation of 1931, one should remember that the initial gains were soon eroded during the course of the 1930s.

The chief economic and financial constraints are discussed in Chapter 3 in the context of a simulated conventional fiscal reflation, and the role of devaluation is also examined. Chapter 4 analyses the longer-term implications of reflation against the background of structural and technological change; while in Chapter 5 some of the regional aspects of unemployment policy are considered. Chapter 6 relates specifically to the 1980s (though not without inter-war parallels) since it deals with unemployment and inflation. The final chapter sums up the argument and looks at the alternatives.

NOTES

1   Comparative data are given in D.H.Aldcroft, *The European Economy* (1980), p.81.
2   For a useful comparative assessment, see W. B. Reddaway, 'The Government's Economic Policy – An Appraisal', *Three Banks Review,* **136** (December 1982).
3   M. Hughes, 'New Dawn for the Sunrise Industries', *Investors Chronicle* (25 February 1983), p.12.
4   R. Turvey, 'Structural Change and Structural Unemployment', International Labour Review, **116** (September – October 1977).
5   The definition of structural unemployment used by many economists (see Turvey above) is too narrow for practical purposes and we have therefore adopted a much wider definition. If structural unemployment is seen simply as a mismatch in the labour market, the extent of which is related to the level of aggregate demand, then on *a priori* grounds one may argue that the mismatch could be alleviated given a sufficiently high level of aggregate demand. However, this solution might simply lead to a temporary concealment of structural unemployment in sectors which are experiencing long-term adverse market forces as specified above. Thus, to give a specific example, government attempts to stimulate artificially the demand for the output of the shipbuilding industry by subsidies, etc. would only serve to maintain employment in that industry at a higher level than was warranted by natural market conditions. In other words, there is always some level of demand which will absorb a labour excess in particular sectors even though it may be structurally unsound in the long-term to do so.
6   R. Kahn, 'Unemployment as Seen by the Keynesians', in G. D. N. Worswick (ed), *The Concept and Measurement of Involuntary Unemployment* (1976), pp.28 – 9. Brittan suggests that Keynes' normal unemployment (non-cyclical) would imply $1\frac{1}{2}$ million on the basis of the labour force of the mid-1970s. S. Brittan, *Second Thoughts on Full Employment Policy* (1975), p.34.
7   W. H. Beveridge, 'An Analysis of Unemployment, III', *Economics,* **4** (1937).
8   M. P. Fogarty, *Prospects of the Industrial Areas of Great Britain* (1945), pp.5, 45
9   The Royal Institute of International Affairs, *Unemployment: An International Problem* (1935), p.57, reckoned that about one-half the unemployment in the years 1931 – 4 could be described as 'depression unemployment'. Unfortunately, they did not define the nature of the remainder.
10 J. Redmond, 'An Indicator of the Effective Exchange Rate of the Pound in the Nineteen-Thirties', *Economic History Review,* **33** (February 1980).
11 C. F. Pratten, 'Mrs Thatcher's Economic Experiment', *Lloyds Bank Review,* **143** (January 1982).

12 University of Warwick, Manpower Research Group, *Review of the Economy and Employment* (Spring 1981), p.117.
13 T. Barker, 'Long-term Recovery. A Return to Full Employment', *Lloyds Bank Review*, **143** (January 1982), p.34, who estimates that 300,000 would be a more realistic figure.
14 *Financial Times*, 4 February 1983
15 B. Hopkin, M. Miller and B. Reddaway, 'An Alternative Economic Strategy – a Message of Hope', *Cambridge Journal of Economics*, **6** (March 1982).
16 See K. Coutts, F. Cripps and T. Ward, 'Britain in the 1980s', *Cambridge Economic Policy Review*, **8** (April 1982).

3 Economic and Financial Constraints to Fiscal Action

In this chapter we shall focus attention on the economic implications of what now would be considered a conventional policy approach to unemployment, that is a fiscal stimulus financed by budget deficits. Despite considerable differences of opinion in recent years with respect to appropriate policy action, demand management may still be regarded as the generally acceptable liberal alternative, and one that is technically capable of generating new employment quickly. Thus many critics of government policy in the 1930s and also recently have advocated a reversal of the restrictive fiscal stance which aggravated the decline in economic activity.[1] Probably the second most readily acceptable policy instrument would be devaluation of the currency, which in the conditions of both the 1930s and 1980s enters the scene as a by-product of fiscal action. Monetary policy, on the other hand, is regarded as more relevant to a spontaneously-induced recovery and therefore will not be considered specifically as a discretionary weapon in this chapter. In any case, its effects in terms of employment generation are both slower and more indirect than those of fiscal policy, and hence it is not generally advocated as a main policy weapon for employment purposes.

WHY LLOYD GEORGE COULD NOT DO IT

Public works as a weapon to combat depression and alleviate unemployment have a long lineage, though their implications from an employment generating point of view were never properly appreciated before 1914. After the war the Labour Party and certain sections of the Liberal Party gave more explicit recognition to the usefulness of public works and from their discussions emerged, albeit in a somewhat loose form, the concept of the multiplier effect of spending and the notion that public works should be deficit financed rather than financed through increased taxation. Much of the limelight in the debate was captured by Lloyd George and his band of supporters who, from the early 1920s, advocated a large-scale programme of public investment as a way of solving Britain's economic difficulties. In actual fact, the Labour movement had already anticipated many of the ideas embodied in the Liberal programme which was launched by Lloyd George in *The Nation and the Athenaeum* in April 1924.[2] The culmination of Liberal thinking came at the end of the decade with the appearance of the Liberal *Yellow Book* in 1928, *Britain's Industrial Future*, which provided the basis for Lloyd George's election manifesto the following year, *We Can Conquer Unemployment*. Its importance lay in the fact that it called for a concerted and positive attack on unemployment and the commitment to a large public works programme. The proposals secured added weight from the approval given to it by Keynes and Henderson in their pamphlet *Can Lloyd George Do It?* In both cases the expediency for deficit financing and the concept of the multiplier effects of government spending were recognised, though certainly not analytically thought out. In fact it was not until two years later that the multiplier concept was explicitly formulated by Kahn in his seminal article in the *Economic Journal*.

Relative to later needs the Lloyd George proposals and the Keynes/Henderson variant were in fact very modest, though one should bear in mind that both were drawn up before the steep rise in unemployment of the early 1930s. The Liberal target was the pre-war unemployment rate of 4.7 per cent, or approximately 570,000 persons as applied to the insured population of the late 1920s. The programme consisted of six major items of spending covering roads, which was by far the largest, housing, telephones, electricity supply, land drainage and London passenger transport. Spending on roads was budgeted at £145 million over a two-year period, followed by telephones and electricity development at £30 million and £31 million respectively. Not all the main programme heads were specified precisely in monetary terms, but from circumstantial evidence it is possible to estimate the total cost of the programme at around £260 million spread over two years and excluding minor works. The employment effects were specified in more detail on the assumption that £1 million worth of expenditure would generate between 4000 and 5000 new jobs (direct and indirect) depending upon the nature of the work carried out. Overall, it was anticipated that the spending incurred in the first year would lead to additional employment of 586,000 which in the second year would rise to 611,000.

Keynes and Henderson in their commentary on the programme accepted most of the premises of the Liberal propositions including the employment implications of the spending exercise, though their analysis was little, if any, more advanced than that contained in the original document. However, they did redefine the amount of expenditure and the time-scale, specifying an annual expenditure of £100 million for three years to give employment to some ½ million workers. It is this variant which has become the accepted version rather than the original Liberal proposals. Moreover, Keynes and Henderson were rather optimistic as to the real or net cost of the programme, believing that up to one-half of the original capital cost would be recouped by a reduction in the costs of unemployment benefit and additional tax revenue as incomes rose through increased economic activity.

On both counts they were probably wide of the mark. Their estimates of job creation from a given volume of expenditure were far too high, though at the time they were made no specific attempt had been made to quantify the impact multiplier. From Kahn's work (1931) onwards it would appear that multiplier values in the range of 2 — 3 were regarded as feasible and certainly Keynes himself later worked with a value around two. However, more recent econometric work on this period suggests that these values were far too high, while no distinction was made between short-run and long-run multipliers. In fact Thomas's short-run income multiplier (one year) is slightly below unity for this period, while the long-run, twelfth period multiplier is only 1.44.[3] Using the intervening values the income and employment changes for the Keynes/Henderson variant of the Lloyd George programme over a period of five years can be calculated.[4] The results are listed in Table 3.1 from which it can be seen that an annual expenditure of £100 million maintained over five years would have led to a reduction of unemployment of 359,000 in the final year as against a rough estimate of 500,000 according to the calculations of Keynes and Henderson and 611,000 after two years under the original Lloyd George programme of some £130 million of expenditure per annum. Thus in terms of the actual unemployment in the terminal year this would have been very small beer indeed.

TABLE 3.1: **Impact of Public Works Expenditure: Keynes/ Henderson Variant of the Lloyd George Programme**

	Actual Unemployment (000s)	*Reduction in Unemployment from the programme (000s)*	*Change in National Income from £100 million increase in Government Spending (£mn)*
1929	1503	268	97.2
1930	2379	300	108.3
1931	3252	329	119.0
1932	3400	346	125.0
1933	3087	359	129.7

Source: T. Thomas, 'Aggregate Demand in the United Kingdom 1918-45', in R. Floud and D. McCloskey (eds), *The Economic History of Britain since 1700*, Vol. 2, *1860 to the 1970s* (1981), p.337.

In other words, the Lloyd George programme would have had to have been multiplied many times over in order to make a serious indentation on the total volume of unemployment at the depth of the depression.[5] Some approximate estimates of the likely order of magnitude can be readily derived by grossing up Thomas's employment generation effects of £1 million of new government spending. If we adopt the maximum twelfth-year impact multiplier of 1.44, then each £1 million of expenditure would produce an increase in employment of 3990 by the final year. Assuming at the extreme the need to create 3 million new jobs, this would have involved a continued annual expenditure of the order of £752 million over a twelve-year period.[6] A lower employment target would of course reduce the total outlay. A lower and more optimistic projection has recently been put forward by Glynn and Howells. Using a short-run multiplier of 1.26 and an average product per capita of 241.65, they calculate that to create 2.8 man years of employment would have required an expenditure of £537 million, derived as follows:

$$\text{Investment spending} = 2.8 \times \frac{241.65}{1.26} = \text{£537 million[7]}$$

These sums are very large, and while they allow for certain leakages into savings and imports, they do not take account fully of the offsets to expenditure through savings on unemployment benefit payments and additional tax revenue as employment incomes rise. Thus the net cost to the budgetary outlay would be somewhat lower and, though it is impossible to specify by how much, it would certainly have been far less than the rough estimate of a half made by Keynes and Henderson. On the other hand, the savings on offsets would not have accrued until activity began to rise so that in the first year or two the total government outlay would have had to have been of the order of magnitude specified. In terms of the budgetary outlays and national income of that period the sums involved are quite massive. For example, the high projection of £752 million is virtually the same as the total national budget in 1932 (£766 million) which in fact recorded a small surplus, while in proportion to the GNP of that year it amounted to no less than 19.3 per cent. Even the lower estimate of Glynn and Howells appears formidable, constituting 13.76 per cent of GNP, 49 per cent of total public authority spending and involving either an increase in government spending or a reduction in revenue equivalent to 70 per cent of the national budget in 1932. Even allowing for some automatic savings in later years the sums are still large, and in any case, what matters is the outlay in the initial years, that is before the revenue offsets begin to bite. As Glynn and Howells point out, 'Even before one asks where the funds to meet the deficit might have come from, the required amount can already be seen to be in the realms of political and economic fantasy.'[8]

On the political side of that there can be no doubt given the commitment to balanced budgets and Treasury opposition to large-scale government spending. There was no question of the National Government resorting to a programme of expenditure of this magnitude, or of any magnitude which necessitated the recourse to deficit financing and further government intervention in the economy. Thus, while there may well have been, as Booth notes, some 'slight softening of the anti-expansionist attitudes' on finance during the course of the 1930s,[9] this was scarcely sufficient to accommodate an expenditure programme of the size required to make serious inroads into the unemployment total. At least until rearmament became a major issue later in the decade and forced the Treasury to modify its traditional stance, the doctrine of minimum government and the innate hostility towards unorthodox economic policies were never seriously challenged.[10] Moreover, apart from the political obstacles there were considerable administrative problems involved in launching a large-scale spending programme, not the least of which centred upon the relationships between the central government and the local authorities with regard to the planning and execution of public works projects.[11] However, irrespective of the political and administrative constraints, there were strong economic and financial reasons why fiscal expansion on this scale could not be contemplated.

The first, and by no means the least important, was simply that of confidence. In the conditions and prevailing beliefs of the time a radical programme involving large-scale state spending would have shattered business and financial confidence. One only has to recall how the prospect of a relatively small budget deficit, which was not premeditated, had given rise to a crisis of confidence in 1931. In that year, when Britain left the gold standard and financial markets everywhere were in a state of turmoil, there was no question of radical experiments being entertained. It was essential, as the Chancellor of the Exchequer (Snowden) was quick to emphasise, to ensure that the country's budgetary position was seen to be sound and that Britain maintained her financial reputation otherwise the consequences for the country and the whole world would be disastrous.[12] Less than a month before the departure from the gold standard Ramsay Macdonald, writing to Edwards, dwelt on the waning confidence in Britain's financial system as the reason why corrective action was imperative:

It is clear that in the midst of the world depression, whatever its causes, fears have arisen abroad as to the stability of our credit and the Budget estimates have fallen short most seriously. If our financial stability is endangered and a run made on our financial resources, the consequences are too terrible to envisage. This makes temporary retrenchment inevitable and imposes some amount of common sacrifice.[13]

Clearly the economic and financial conditions of the early 1930s precluded any radical departure from orthodoxy in the eyes of contemporaries. In the event Britain's financial institutions, unlike those of many other countries, emerged unscathed from the events of 1931, and the government's relentless pursuit of financial orthodoxy did much to restore confidence both at home and abroad. Was the climate not more favourable therefore once the crisis conditions had passed? Apparently not, according to the Chancellor's (Neville Chamberlain's) budgetary stance; he combined 'experience and orthodoxy' and regarded sound financial policy (balanced budgets) as a prerequisite for recovery and the maintenance of continued confidence in Britain's economic and financial system. Moreover, Chamberlain asserted that by following sound financial principles it had been possible to secure lower interest rates which were regarded as essential to economic recovery.[14] In the latter respect the Chancellor had a point to his credit, but he probably exaggerated the influence of cheap money on recovery as well as the dangers of any departure from sound finance. A moderate fiscal boost through deficit financing may not have proved too harmful by the mid-1930s when conditions had stabilised, but by then of course a strong and spontaneous recovery was well under way. On the other hand, a radical programme on the scale outlined above could never have been contemplated. The canons of financial rectitude were so deeply engrained within society that any attempt to resort to large-scale deficit financing would have created renewed worries about Britain's financial integrity, the strength of the currency, fear of inflation, however unjustified, and led to a flight of capital, which together could have brought back 'the nightmare of recession'.[15]

Some of these fears may have been unfounded, but in times of difficulty, as in the 1980s, the cautionary instinct tends to gain the upper hand which effectively closes the door to bold and enterprising action. Accordingly, the Cabinet was content to rely on

natural forces and the restoration of investor confidence not because anyone thought that was the quickest way to reduce unemployment, but because ministers believed that it was the approach which provided the best balance of recovery and stability, with the former having no priority over the latter.[16]

In one respect therefore the government's fiscal policy in the 1930s may be regarded as successful in that it helped to restore confidence. As we know, in terms of modern definitions of the targets and objectives of budgetary policy, the fiscal stance during the 1930s was restrictive and destabilising. Though public investment and local authority spending were maintained and even increased through to 1931, thereby partly offsetting the central government's deflationary action and the drop in private sector capital formation, the financial crisis of that year inevitably led to a sharp reversal of total public spending in subsequent years as economy campaigns were pushed through. Thus in the years 1931-4 there was a large, constant employment budget surplus. It was not until recovery was well under way that there was any relaxation and the constant employment budgetary surplus was only eliminated in 1937. In the modern sense of the term, therefore, budgetary policy was anything but stabilising. On the other hand, in so far as adherence to budgetary orthodoxy provided a stable environment for business, restored investor confidence after the traumatic crisis of 1931, and paved the way for an easier monetary policy, then budgetary policy can be considered successful.[17] Indeed, the fact that a strong, sustained and largely spontaneous recovery set in at an early date in Britain and that it was more vigorous than in many other major countries, would tend to lend some support to the importance of restoring business and investor confidence by sound national financial policies.

One of the fears expressed about deficit financing at the time was that it would lead to inflation. This might seem rather unwarranted at a time of collapsing prices and under-utilised resources, but it derived from two sources: first, the recollection of the dramatic European inflations of the early 1920s which were regarded as being largely a product of reckless spending by governments; and secondly, the possibility, however remote, that any deficit generated by an expansionary fiscal programme would be financed in an inflationary way, either by printing money or by short-term bank borrowing, a sufficient guarantee of undermining confidence. It is unlikely however that the government would have reduced the Bank of England's control over the money market in the same way that it had done in the early post-war years. The Bank of England itself was opposed to unbalanced budgets, not, as Sayers points out, due to any specific 'Gladstonian fetish' in strict budgetary orthodoxy, but simply because it wished to ensure that there was no repetition of the uncontrolled credit expansion of 1919-20 when it had lost control over the market.[18] The Treasury, moreover, having funded most of the short-term debt arising from the war and carried through a successful conversion operation in 1932, was in no mood to contemplate the prospects of the exercise having to be repeated again. The main alternative — that of funding the prospective deficit — also presented its own problems and indirectly it would have had deflationary implications on the monetary side.

In the first instance the chief problem was the size of the national debt and the costs of servicing it. Most of this had been generated by the first world war and throughout the 1920s and early 1930s the Treasury was busy trying to reduce the overall burden of debt and its servicing costs, while at the same time funding the large post-war floating debt. During the first post-war decade debt interest accounted for around one-third or more of public spending and some 7 per cent of GNP, and though after the 1932 conversion operation the interest burden declined it still remained very high (indeed somewhat greater than in the 1970s) compared with the pre-1914 period[19] when debt servicing costs accounted for a negligible proportion of public spending and national income. In practical terms, therefore, 'The size of the debt as a problem *per se* would weigh in the policy regardless of whether projected government borrowing were to be financed by Treasury Bills or issues of stock.'[20]

But the preoccupation with restraining the size of the national debt was not the only impediment to new financing. The fact is that the authorities experienced some difficulty in selling stock in the 1930s and consequently had large additional quantities of gilt-edged stock been unleashed on an unwilling market, some inducement would have to have been offered to tempt buyers. When rates of interest were reduced to a minimum after the War Loan Conversion of 1932, the authorities effectively blocked the market in government stock. Thus to entice buyers to accept more stock it would have been necessary to raise long-term interest rates since, with Bank Rate at a floor of 2 per cent, anticipated interest rates were in an upward direction which would have meant a capital loss on gilt purchases had they been bought at the then prevailing level of interest rates. In fact, during the course of the 1930s long-term rates were tending to move upwards even though the government's funding operations were quite small. Thus deficit financing would have pushed up rates further and increased the costs of servicing the national debt. Moreover, higher interest rates would have exerted a deflationary impact on the economy, especially in the residential housing market, one of the main beneficiaries of low interest rates and one of the main contributors to recovery in the 1930s.

The next issue to consider is how the external account would have stood up to a fiscal expansion. Experience since 1945 suggests that rising incomes and domestic activity tend to lead to a deterioration in the balance of payments partly because of the large leakage into imports. This is in contrast to the experience in the nineteenth century when the current account of the balance of payments improved during booms and deteriorated in recessions. The inter-war years appear to have marked a transitional period towards the post-1945 pattern. Thus Thomas estimates that even Lloyd George's modest programme of spending would have resulted in an adverse shift in the current account balance of between £20-25 million, and this is assuming a relatively low marginal propensity to import of 0.208.[21] As we have seen it would have been necessary to have increased this programme several times for it to have been realistic in terms of the unemployment problem. Taking an upper bound spending programme and making allowances for increasing supply inelasticities and upward price shifts as domestic activity increased, then the deterioration in the current account balance could have been on the upper side of £150 million. Furthermore, the combination of an adverse current balance and unbalanced budgets would have caused a capital outflow and thereby weakened the capital account of the balance of payments.

Could the external account have been squared by a devaluation of sterling?[22] It should first be pointed out that, other things being equal, devaluation as such was not a policy option open to the authorities in the 1930s since the upward pressure on the currency in this period was difficult to resist given the uncertainty in international financial markets at this time. Of course, under a big fiscal programme and accompanying deterioration in the current account balance this problem would have been removed, and so it would not have been difficult to engineer a downward shift of the sterling exchange rate under the managed float of the 1930s. However, there is some doubt as to whether devaluation would have been effective in terms of improving the balance of payments since the sum of the import and export price elasticities was a little below unity (0.95), whereas to be effective it must exceed unity. Moreover, since we are assuming unilateral fiscal action, presumably prices and costs would eventually have risen relative to those abroad thus worsening Britain's competitive position. Hence short of foreign borrowing, which is difficult under these conditions and can be ruled out as a permanent solution, the only way of securing external equilibrium would have been increasing controls on various components of the balance of payments.

Some of the more specific implications of a general fiscal thrust — structural and regional — are appropriately considered in subsequent chapters. For the moment we may summarise the position for the 1930s as follows. While we know that the political and economic thought processes of the time presented an effective barrier to revolutionary policy-making in the 1930s, it must also be recognised that irrespective of these factors there were serious economic and financial constraints which would have circumscribed any large-scale programme of spending to mop up unemployment. In fact, as long ago as 1944 H.W. Arndt was mindful of the balance of payments constraint and felt that this alone would have necessitated resort to a controlled economy along the lines of the German model had deficit spending on the scale required been introduced. 'An expansionist policy would ... in all probability ... have meant the transformation of the British economy into a largely State-controlled, if not planned, economic system.'[23] Moreover, when we take into account the structural and regional aspects of the unemployment problem, the relevance of a generalised Keynesian fiscal thrust becomes even more attenuated. Indeed, given the impotency of fiscal measures to alter materially the structural parameters of the economy, the scope for fiscal action was very limited.

By way of addendum it may be interesting to consider briefly the findings of one of the earliest quantitative assessments of full employment which was drafted by Nicholas Kaldor and published as an appendix to Beveridge's *Full Employment in a Free Society* (1944). Since the base year adopted was 1938 the employment generation target is much lower at 1.25 million, on the assumption that 97 per cent of the workforce should be employed. Kaldor estimated that this would require an 11 per cent increase in output on 1938 and he specified three alternative routes to achieve this full employment outlay, as follows:

1 Government expenditure is raised to secure outlay with tax rates unchanged from the 1938 level.
2 Government expenditure is kept at the 1938 level, but the total tax yield is reduced to allow the requisite expansion in private outlay.

48

3   Government revenue is kept equal to expenditure (no borrowing) but both are increased to the level required to secure full employment outlay.

Even with this lower employment target, the budgetary and balance of payments impact is found to be quite severe. Approaches 1 and 2 involve deficit financing and public outlays out of loans, estimated at £230 million and £340 million respectively. Under alternative 3, there is no borrowing and activity is generated through the balanced budget multiplier. This therefore necessitates a very large increase in spending — in fact no less than £910 million, which on the actual public outlay in 1938 (£725 million) would have resulted in public expenditure more than doubling. Moreover, since revenue must rise to match expenditure, tax rates would have to be raised by 66 per cent across the board, or by no less than 94 per cent if confined solely to direct taxation. Clearly the last alternative would have been a non-starter politically, while even the first two would have imposed severe strains on the financial system. The balance of payments impact was also far from negligible. Kaldor estimates the full employment adverse balance at £130 million as against the actual deficit of £55 million in 1938. To square the external account exports would need to rise by 25 per cent or imports cut by 15 per cent on the hypothetical full employment level, or a combination of both.

REFLATIONARY PROSPECTS IN THE 1980S

Macro-economic policy of the last few years has some of the principal features of that of the 1930s. The main economic objectives of the Conservative Government elected in May 1979, were to lower the rate of inflation and to create the right conditions for sustainable growth of output and employment.[24] In accordance with the new Tory economic philosophy, the traditional postwar macro-policy of demand management was rejected on the grounds that it was partly responsible for the 'stagflation' of the mid-1970s onwards, and that it would not solve the problems of the 1980s. Instead, strict monetary and fiscal policies were to be implemented to bring down the rate of inflation, while the conditions for sustained growth were to be laid by means of a supply side strategy.[25] The latter would reflect the Tory belief in freedom of enterprise and markets and the importance of incentives. Accordingly, controls over prices, dividends, industrial location, the exchange and labour markets would be abolished or liberalised, subsidies would be phased out, while lower taxes and a shift from direct to indirect taxation would restore incentives to enterprise and individual initiative.[26]

Much of the policy programme has since been implemented, though in the early years of the administration the monetary and fiscal targets fell wide of the mark, and hence inflation remained high, indeed it rose sharply for a time. Subsequently, macro-policy was tightened considerably and inflation fell rapidly, helped for a time by a strong exchange rate, but the side-effects in terms of lost output and jobs were far greater than the government anticipated. Nevertheless, the government continues to stick to its central macro-targets and policies in the belief that spontaneous recovery will soon emerge.

What then is the alternative? Would a general fiscal thrust be any more viable now than in the 1930s, or could a similar scenario be written for the present? The position is perhaps a little more complicated today, given the larger range of policy options available and the differing projections made as to the effects of alternative policies to those currently in force. However, we may at this stage simplify matters by sticking to a conventional reflationary package via the budget coupled with devaluation, the latter following automatically by virtue of the free float of sterling. This is also consistent with the views of many of the critics of government policy who maintain that a significant fiscal stimulus is required to reverse the downward slide in output and to create new employment. The general assumption is that the fiscal boost would be financed by a rising public sector deficit rather than by taxation.

Since estimates of the impact on employment of changes in government spending or revenue vary considerably, partly depending upon the nature of the changes made, the following data should be regarded only as broad orders of magnitude of the impact effects. As a rough approximation, a £1 billion increase in government spending or reduction in revenue through tax cuts will generate approximately 50,000 jobs if maintained over a period of two to three years. Assuming, therefore, the target is to provide work for about 3 million persons then the expenditure requirement would be in the region of £60 billion. The net cost and rise in the public sector financial deficit would be less than this amount since there would be offsets through reduced social welfare benefits and increased tax revenues as economic activity and employment rise, amounting to between £12-13 billion at 1981-2 prices.[27] Hence the total outlay involved in absorbing the current unemployment would be approximately £47-8 billion, though this of course makes no allowance for the natural increase in the labour force.

These estimates are large, but they are far from being over-generous. In April 1981 the *Cambridge Economic Policy Review* calculated that even to stabilise the level of unemployment at 2½ million would require a growth rate of GDP of 3 per cent per annum, and a public sector deficit of £20 — 30 billion, together with a controlled devaluation of between 5-10 per cent per annum. Thus to secure full employment would require either a much larger spending programme and deficit, or faster depreciation of the currency, or both in order to raise the growth of GDP well above 3 per cent a year.[28]

In fact, given the magnitude of the problem, it is very doubtful whether conventional policies to cure unemployment would be viable in terms of the constraints of financial stability, balance of payments equilibrium and price stability. In the words of the Cambridge Economic Policy Group, 'Within the range of what could conceivably be described as conventional policies, there is no longer any strategy left which would now rescue the economy from the appalling condition to which it has been brought by the policies followed since North Sea oil came on stream.'[29] This is the main reason why the Group have constantly advocated import and exchange controls to counter the situation. While we would not fully share their pessimism or their predilection for controls, there is little doubt that Keynesian policies advocated by critics of government policy would have serious consequences. Some indication of the implications for key economic variables can be seen in the Appendix to this chapter, which contains projections on the basis of the Labour Party's recent proposals for expansion.

A massive reflationary programme, or even a moderate one for that matter, would undoubtedly have serious implications for the financial and money markets, sterling, the balance of payments and inflation, and it is doubtful whether it could be maintained for very long in the absence of controls. On the financial side it would almost certainly cause a panic, leading to a flight of capital assuming the absence of exchange controls, while it would inevitably lead to a rise in interest rates – with deflationary consequences – in order for the government to be able to sell huge volumes of new debt. The situation would be very similar to the one described for the 1930s. As Tomlinson has stressed, budget deficits cannot be manipulated at will by governments bent on pursuing the dictates of demand management. The crucial issue therefore is not an ideological one determined by the political complexion of the Party in power, but rather the restraint imposed by the market's (financial institutions) response to the size and direction of public expenditure and public deficits.

Under arrangements where government deficits are financed by selling debt to private institutions then what matters is the conception these institutions hold of appropriate government policy, irrespective of what [some] economists might say was for example a proper governmental response to recession.[30]

The leverage which the financial market can exercise over government policy is well illustrated by the gilt 'buyers' strike' in 1976 when the market judged the prevailing level of interest rates to be too low given the increasing risks engendered by large public deficits, high inflation and the collapse of sterling. Funding came to a standstill as gilt buyers took fright, and the authorities were forced to flood the market with short-term paper, at further inflationary cost. A receptive market was not restored until interest rates were raised and the government showed signs of moving towards financial rectitude by imposing expenditure cuts.

Whether the actions of the financial markets in this type of situation are regarded as justified or not, the fact remains that they can dictate the terms on which the government funds its debt. In these circumstances governments with large spending programmes are forced to offer the market substantial induce-ments in the form of higher interest rates if they are to stand any change of funding substantial deficits. Hence the Duke of York tactic adopted in the 1970s of raising interest rates to the top of the hill and then bringing them down again, at which point gilt buyers are tempted back into the market. The only problem is that each time the exercise is repeated the peak of the hill gets higher with a consequent ratchet-effect on interest rates. In practice, of course, higher interest rates will have a deflationary impact and therefore partly offset the fiscal leverage. The alternative to funding would be to issue short-term debt (bank borrowing through Treasury Bills) or to print money, but these methods would have inflationary impli-cations because of the effects on the money supply.

Clearly then financial markets, whose basic philosophy is of a monetarist persuasion, can exercise considerable pressure to restrain governments with reckless spending proclivities. In a wider context, Andrea Boltho has drawn attention to the way that shifts in private sector behaviour in response to policy changes can frustrate or reduce the effectiveness of such policies; he also notes how recent inflationary packages in France have been impaired 'by unfavourable expectations of the ultimate impact of such policies held by financial markets', thereby forcing the French government to reverse its policy stance.[31]

As far as the balance of payments and inflation are con-cerned, any fiscal boost would tend to have adverse effects on both counts, though much depends on the reaction of sterling and the level of economic activity in the rest of the world. The most unfavourable outcome for the balance of payments would be a situation in which unilateral expansionary mea-sures were adopted and sterling remained fixed. Given Britain's weak competitive trading position, which is reflected in the country's unfavourable trade elasticities,[32] any domestic expansion would be followed by a surge in imports, especially of manufactures,[33] unmatched by a similar increase in exports, thus giving rise eventually to a huge balance of payments deficit. Even under a controlled downward float of sterling of between 5-10 per cent a year, assuming this were possible, the overall deficit on the balance of payments, including capital flows, would be large, possibly rising to between £10-15 billion over a 2-3 year period.[34] However, neither of these versions is very plausible since under a floating exchange sterling in all probability would collapse from the impact of the reflationary measures. In turn this would ease the pressure on the balance of payments, assuming favourable demand and supply elasticities for tradeable commodities.[35] In practice, however, the improvement in the external account would be offset by outward capital flows as sterling holders try to get out of the currency, the narrowing of margins by importers to compensate for the depreciation of sterling, and the domestic inflationary effects of sterling's fall. In other words, the counterpart to partial relief to the balance of payments would be more domestic inflation. Import prices would rise rapidly and feed through to the domestic price level which in turn would influence money wage settlements unless these could be contained by some form of control, and past experience does not hold out a great deal of hope on this score. Price inflation would quickly rise again into double figures and there is no guarantee that once started the acceleration could be checked easily.

Thus the balance of payments and/or price constraints effectively block a full employment policy, assuming a *ceteris paribus* condition. Despite the bonus of North Sea oil, to generate sufficient growth to absorb 3 million unemployed would result in insupportable payments deficits, assuming a fixed or modest fall in the exchange rate, while devaluation on the scale required to cope with the latter would lead to unacceptable rates of inflation. The best one could aim for might be a modest inflationary package which would contain the damage to the balance of payments and inflation, but which would do little more than stabilise unemployment around the current level. Indeed, even this might prove ambitious given the continued growth in the labour force and further manpower losses through efficiency gains as manufacturing industry strives to strengthen its competitiveness.

On the other hand, it might be argued that the current balance of payments surplus could provide the basis of a reflationary stimulus of some magnitude with favourable effects in terms of output and jobs. Unfortunately the impact would be short-lived since despite the contribution of North Sea oil the full employment balance of payments is in serious deficit as a result of the serious structural defects of the economy. Reflation may therefore provide a year or two of reasonable growth, but it cannot by itself solve the structural defects of the economy. Thus, apart from the fact that

any significant expansion would run the risk of undermining financial confidence both at home and abroad [and] in the absence of exchange controls, the danger of initiating an uncontrollable fall in sterling and unleashing renewed inflationary pressure is a very real one ... [it cannot] improve export growth or slow down import penetration. Once Britain's balance of payments is again in deficit the growth of domestic expenditure will be constrained, as in the past, by inadequate trade performance in manufacturing. Reflation may check industrial decline but it will not of itself put the process into reverse. Strategies for recovery need to be judged as much in terms of their ability to accomplish this task as in terms of their likely effect on output and employment in the short term.[36]

The longer-term structural problem is the crux of the matter and a reflationary package to secure a temporary boost to employment may in fact exacerbate, and at best do little to alleviate, the very constraints which it runs up against. A full employment growth rate cannot be achieved because of the balance of payments constraint and this in turn is caused by the unfavourable structural parameters of the British economy, and industry in particular, which make for a weak competitive position in home and export markets. Whatever its derivatives, be it high costs, low productivity, or inability to compete in non-price terms or a combination of all three, the fact remains that a major fiscal reflation will not solve these defects. Indeed, it could aggravate them in so far as government spending is concentrated on public works and public services, which have a low propensity to export, provide little import substitution and where productivity growth is low. Moreover, any sudden domestic income gains would leak rapidly into imports because of short-term supply bottlenecks in products with a high income elasticity of demand, for example, consumer durables.

It is because of these inherent difficulties that the Cambridge Group of economists advocate protection for the external account in the form of import and exchange controls alongside reflationary policies and devaluation. However, they do not explain how to avoid the inflationary implications of devaluation, nor do they convincingly demonstrate how their policy package, which in effect shelters domestic industry from international competition, would achieve a marked improvement in the structural parameters of the economy. If anything, it could lead to an ossification of the industrial structure and a further deterioration in Britain's competitive strength which is the source of the problem in the first place. This issue is considered more fully in Chapter 4.

CONCLUSION

It is difficult to see therefore how, either in the 1930s or in the present situation, a major reflation to generate employment on the scale required could be implemented without running into severe economic and financial constraints. These constraints would be the more severe if Britain took action unilaterally, less so if other major countries inflated at the same time. In short, the unfavourable structural features of the economy set a limit to the sustainable rate of growth which falls well short of that required to achieve full employment. In fact, the sustainable rate of growth of GDP over the medium term is probably 2 per cent or less, scarcely sufficient to stabilise unemployment at its present level, whereas a growth rate of two to three times this amount would be required to get anywhere near to previous full employment levels. Begg and Rhodes, for example, calculate that to reduce unemployment by 1 million in the remainder of the decade would require a growth in manufacturing output of about 5 per cent a year.[37] Any attempt to move towards a full employment growth rate would very soon lead to financial instability and undermine the goals of external equilibrium and price stability (in the present context a non-accelerating rate of inflation). The consequence would be a renewed bout of fiscal and monetary restriction to rescue the situation and the final outcome might be even higher unemployment.

A further consideration to bear in mind in the current situation is that a given reflationary stimulus may have lower output effects and higher price effects than the proponents of government spending anticipate. This stems in part from the specific structural weaknesses of the British economy, but it also reflects the increasing supply inelasticities which, for various reasons, have developed in western economies over the last decade,[38] and which cannot be solved by reflation. Thus unless it can be shown that a reflationary stimulus will materially assist the necessary structural transformation of the economy – which we very much doubt given the conventional format of such policies – then it is debatable whether, in view of the known economic and financial constraints, it is worth the risk.

It does not follow from the above comments that demand management has outlived its usefulness.[39] Some modest relaxation of the current fiscal stance (and the same goes for the 1930s) could be beneficial to activity without running into serious constraints, but of course it would not cure unemployment which is the problem under discussion here. However, it should be stressed that it is misleading to assume that the experience of the 1950s and 1960s can provide a guide to policy action today. Contrary to popular conception, fiscal policy in that period was never called upon to do more than make marginal adjustments to an economy which was sustained by strong growth forces, albeit they were weaker than in most other countries. Full employment and sustained growth were the product of real growth forces and not Keynesian employment policies which were never really put to the test in the sense of large-scale deficit financing to deal with a massive unemployment problem. In fact, for most of the period through to the mid-1970s, budgets were persistently in surplus on current account and fiscal policy was largely a matter of adjusting the size of the surplus through taxes rather than by expenditure manipulation. In other words, demand management was successful only because it had to deal with small deviations from full employment in a growing economy.[40] Once the favourable conditions disappeared and the unemployment problem deepened fiscal policy was incapable of generating sustained recovery and full employment in an economy whose structural parameters had deteriorated over time and against a background of weak real growth forces in the world economy at large, without running up against the severe constraints outlined in this chapter.[41] In the next chapter therefore we shall examine some of the ways in which reflationary employment policies may retard the process of structural and technological change on which Britain's future depends.

APPENDIX

Labour's Strategy for Unemployment

The implications of the Labour Party's recent proposals for dealing with unemployment have been examined in detail by the Henley Centre for Forecasting and they bear out the points discussed in this chapter. Projections are made on the basis of an £11 billion reflationary programme carried out over a period of 18 months, with an initial reduction in VAT by 2½ percentage points and no incomes policy. The forecasts show that after an initial fillip to output and a modest reduction in unemployment, the policy runs up against the familiar constraints. By 1985, when it is assumed the policy will be abandoned, earnings and prices growth are well into double figures, the balance of payments is in serious deficit, the public sector borrowing requirement is more than double the present level, while interest rates have soared back to 17 per cent. Subsequently, under a reversed policy stance the initial improvement in growth is undermined and unemployment creeps upwards once again. Even under an alternative projection, with some form of incomes control and an expansion programme spread over a number of years, unemployment remains above 2 million, and by 1987 inflation is approaching double figures.

TABLE 3.2: **Projections on Labour's £11 billion Expansion Programme**

	1983	*1984*	*1985*	*1986*	*1987*
Real GDP (per cent)	2.1	3.6	2.6	1.1	1.0
Retail Price Index (per cent)	6.8	10.2	14.0	15.1	13.3
Unemployment (million)	3.0	2.9	2.7	2.7	2.8
PSBR (£ bn)	16.0	20.0	22.0	23.0	24.0
Balance of payments (£ bn)	-0.2	-3.1	-4.5	-1.6	-0.4
Interest rates (per cent)	8.0	12.0	17.0	16.0	14.0
Effective exchange rate (trade weighted)	73.0	68.0	61.0	58.0	55.0

Source: Henley Centre for Forecasting.

NOTES

1 Data on the fiscal stance in the 1930s and from the mid-1970s is given in R. Middleton, 'The Constant Employment Budget Balance and British Budgetary Policy, 1929-39', *Economic History Review*, **34** (1981); and J. Tomlinson, 'Unemployment and Policy in the 1930s and 1980s', *Three Banks Review,* **135** (September 1982).

2 For the antecedents, see D. I. Mackay, D. J. Forsyth and D. M. Kelly, 'The Discussion of Public Works Programmes, 1917 – 1935: Some Reflections on the Labour Movement's Contribution', *International Review of Social History*, **11** (1966).

3 It is interesting to note that the income multiplier in Nazi Germany was also relatively low at around 1.5, which Overy attributes in part to the fact that private activity did not respond as expected to increased public spending and that government money was simply a substitute for money that would otherwise have been generated through the private capital market, and partly to the rather poor productivity performance of the German economy through 1929 – 38 on account of the large share of resources poured into areas of low productive potential such as armaments, roadbuilding and construction. R. J. Overy, *The Nazi Economic Recovery, 1932 – 1938* (1982), pp.43 – 4.

4 There is some confusion in the reporting on the various proposals for increased state spending. The Liberal *Yellow Book* proposed a programme over five years, but the main heads of expenditure in the 1929 election manifesto were to be implemented within a two-year period,

with no clear indication of what was to follow. The total spending per year in the latter document is not made clear, but it probably amounted to around £130 million per annum on the basis of the details specified. Keynes and Henderson, in *Can Lloyd George Do It?*, outlined a three-year programme of £100 million a year, which Thomas has extended to five years.

5   Lloyd George later revised his spending programme to £400 million and found support from a most unlikely source, namely Philip Snowden, former Labour Chancellor of the Exchequer, whose conversion to 'unsound' finance owed much to his personal antipathy to Ramsay Macdonald rather than to any rational process of thought. See Lord Snowden, *Mr. Lloyd George's New Deal* (1935); and C. Cross, *Philip Snowden* (1966), pp.337 – 9.

6   T. Thomas, *Aspects of U.K. Mcroeconomic Policy during the Interwar Period: A Study in Econometric History*, University of Cambridge PhD (1975), pp.188, 225

7   S. Glynn and P. G. A. Howells, 'Unemployment in the 1930s: The Keynesian Solution Reconsidered', *Australian Economic History Review*, **20** (1980), p.41.

8   Ibid., p.42.

9   A. Booth, 'The Keynesian Revolution in Economic Policy-making', *Economic History Review*, **36** (1983), p.123; see also, S. Howson and D. Winch, *The Economic Advisory Council, 1930 – 1939: A Study in Economic Advice during Depression and Recovery* (1977).

10   For a good up-to-date survey of these matters, see W. R. Garside, 'The Failure of the Radical Alternative: Public Works, Deficit Finance and British Interwar Unemployment', *Journal of European Economic History* (1983): see also R. Skidelsky, 'Keynes and the Treasury View: The Case for and against an Active Unemployment Policy, 1920 – 1939', in W. J. Mommsen (ed.), *The Emergence of the Welfare State in Britain and Germany, 1850 – 1950* (1981), pp.185 – 6.

11   These aspects are covered in Garside, *loc. cit.*: and R. Middleton, 'The Treasury in the 1930s: Political and Administrative Constraints to Acceptance of the New Economics', *Oxford Economic Papers*, **34** (1982).

12   R. Bassett, *Nineteen Thirty-One Political Crisis* (1958), pp.45 – 6.

13   R. Macdonald to E. Edwards, MP, 25 August 1931.

14   B. E. V. Sabine, *British Budgets in Peace and War, 1932 – 1945* (1970), pp.15 – 16, 299.

15   Ibid., p.299.

16   F. C. Miller, 'The Unemployment Policy of the National Government, 1931 – 1936', *The Historical Journal*, **19** (1976) p.476. According to Garside the government was determined not to upset the 'natural' forces of recovery by expansionist and interventionist policies which threatened to weaken the restorative influence of the slump in purging the system of 'unsound' investment and unproductive practices. Garside, *loc. cit.*

17   R. Middleton, 'The Constant Employment Budget Balance and British

Budgetary Policy, 1929 – 39' *Economic History Review*, **34** (May 1981), pp.283 – 6; N. H. Dimsdale, 'British Monetary Policy and the Exchange Rate, 1920 – 1938', *Oxford Economic Papers*, Supplement (1981), p.340.

18   R. S. Sayers, *The Bank of England, 1891* – 1944, vol 1 (1976), p.224
19   For comparative data see Middleton (1982), *loc. cit.*, p.54; and *Financial Times*, 24 February 1983.
20   J. D. Tomlinson, 'Unemployment and Government Policy between the Wars: A Note', *Journal of Contemporary History*, **13** (1978), p.72.
21   Thomas (1975), *op. cit.*
22   We recognise that sterling was devalued in 1931 and here refer to a further devaluation in the knowledge that by the mid-1930s the effective sterling rate was back to the 1929 level. See J. Redmond, 'An Indicator of the Effective Exchange Rate of the Pound in the Nineteen-Thirties', *Economic History Review*, **33** (February 1980).
23   H. W. Arndt, *Economic Lessons of the Nineteen-Thirties* (1944, 1963 reprint), pp.134 – 5. Nazi spending policies required extensive controls over the whole economy to make the system work. See Overy, *op. cit.*, p.51.
24   See R. C. O. Matthews and W. B. Reddaway, 'Can Mrs Thatcher Do It?', *Midland Bank Review*, (Autumn 1980).
25   The defeat of inflation was also regarded as a prerequisite for sustained growth.
26   W. B. Reddaway, 'The Government's Economic Policy – An Appraisal', *Three Banks Review*, **136** (December 1982).
27   A. W. Dilnot and C. N. Morris, 'The Exchequer Costs of Unemployment', *Fiscal Studies*, **2** (November 1981), p.17.
28   *Cambridge Economic Policy Review*, **7** (April 1981), p.23.
29   Ibid., p.24.
30   J. Tomlinson, 'Why Was There Never a Keynesian Revolution in Economic Policy?', *Economy and Society*, **10** (February 1981), pp.83 – 5.
31   A. Boltho, 'Is Western Europe Caught in an Expectations Trap?', *Lloyds Bank Review*, **148** (April 1983), p.8.
32   The UK income elasticity of demand for imports is about 1.6 and the income elasticity of demand for UK exports around unity. See A. P. Thirlwall, 'The UK's Economic Problems: A Balance of Payments Constraint?', *National Westminster Bank Quarterly Review* (February 1978), p.17.
33   Every 1 per cent by which British spending rises, imports rise by some 3 – 4 per cent. *Investors Chronicle*, 3 December 1982, p.572.
34   *Cambridge Economic Policy Review*, (April 1981), p.23
35   It has been questioned whether devaluation is an effective remedy for this purpose given the unfavourable elasticities of demand for exports and imports, though it should be noted that the price elasticities are somewhat better than the income elasticities. Thirlwall, *loc. cit.*, and C. M. Cooper and J. A. Clark, *Employment, Economics and Technology* (1982), pp.34 – 5, 39.

36   *Cambridge Economic Policy Review*, **8** (April 1982), pp.1 – 2.
37   I. Begg and J. Rhodes, 'Will British Industry Recover?', *Cambridge Economic Policy Review*, **8** (April 1982), p.25.
38   See H. Giersch, 'Aspects of Growth, Structural Change and Employment – A Schumpeterian Perspective,' *Weltwirtschaftliches Archiv.*, **115** (1979).
39   See G. D. N. Worswick, 'The End of Demand Mangement', *Lloyds Bank Review*, **123** (January 1977); and more recently, A. P. Thirlwall, 'Keynesian Employment Theory is not Defunct', *Three Banks Review*, **131** (September 1981).
40   See R. C. O. Matthews, 'Why has Britain had Full Employment since the War?' *Economic Journal*, **78** (1968); and Tomlinson, *Economy and Society* (1981), *loc. cit.*, pp.120 – 1, 134.
41   Professor Thirlwall, in *The Three Banks Review* (September 1981), rises to the defence of Keynesian employment policy but he does not explain how this would solve Britain's main structural constraint, namely that of converting more resources into foreign exchange to improve the non-oil balance of payments. For a detailed exposition of the balance of payments constraint in the post-war period, see his *Balance of Payments Theory and United Kingdom Experience* (1980); see also J. Meade, 'A New Keynesian Approach to Full Employment', *Lloyds Bank Review*, **150** (October 1983).

4 Technical Change, Structural Transformation and Jobless Growth

So far we have discussed the chief macro-economic constraints to a policy of full employment. We now turn to the real side of the economy and examine the structural factors underlying the unemployment. It has already been noted that a large part of the present unemployment derives from the manufacturing sector, and it is the contention here that much of this can be seen as a facet of a major structural shift or transformation in the composition of output. It has been caused by both secular and cyclical forces as well as supply-side shocks and most major industrial economies have been affected to varying degrees. The result of these changes is to produce a mismatch of employment opportunities in the labour market which cannot readily be alleviated by conventional demand management policies.

TECHNICAL OPPORTUNITIES

Following Cornwall, Maddison and Rostow, it may justifiably be argued that the dynamic sector in the super-growth of the 1950s and 1960s was manufacturing whose rate of growth far outstripped that of either agriculture or services.[1] Since the early 1970s the reverse has been the case; manufacturing ceased to be the engine of growth, its employment declined, while the rate of output growth of the service sector, though lower than hitherto, exceeded that of manufacturing industry by a substantial margin. Two points are worthy of emphasis:

during the 1970s the generation of employment opportunities in services was insufficient to compensate for the large shake-out of labour from industry; secondly, despite secular expansion, industry's employment generating capacity was dwindling steadily over time; for the nine EEC countries, combined industrial employment rose by 1 per cent per annum in the period 1950 – 1965 while output of the sector increased by 7 per cent annually; by 1965 – 73 employment was more or less static despite a 6 per cent growth in output, while after 1973 industrial output rose very slowly (around 1 per cent per annum) and employment fell at a rate approaching 2 per cent a year.[2] In other words, indsutry is now experiencing what agriculture has had for many years, namely jobless growth, and there has been some suggestion that this pattern may spread to the service sector in due course as a result of technical change (see below).

These trends are familiar to most western industrial economies though more pronounced in the case of Britain due to specific parochial factors which will be discussed separately later. They cannot be attributed solely to cyclical disturbances and the exogenous shocks of the 1970s, since their presence pre-dates these events, though the latter certainly accentuated the secular changes taking place. It is important therefore to determine why manufacturing ceased to be an engine of growth and became a job loser, and also whether services are likely to share the same fate in due course.

One possibility is that investment opportunities deteriorated over time as a result of the diminishing scope for technological innovation and diffusion. Several authors have drawn attention to the possibility of an apparent technological gap thereby reviving in the process the Schumpeterian notion that innovations tend to cluster in point of time and thus create a bunching of investment opportunities in particular periods. Mensch, for example, points to the lack of significant or basic innovations in the last decade or so,[3] while Giarini and Loubergé see the crisis in economic growth in terms of the weakening of the technological cycle.[4] In a rather more rigorous analysis, Freeman and his co-authors likewise stress the uneven nature of technical change over time as between industries and sectors of the economy, and the inherent lumpiness in the thrust of new technological systems. This process leads to a swarming effect in terms of investment and employment as technological diffusion takes place, but in time the employment consequences tend to weaken. Employment generation per unit of investment declines as a result of scale effects, the decline in profit margins as new firms enter the field, and the increasing saturation of markets for products of the existing technological system. Once this stage is reached the problem becomes one of making the leap to a new technological system, the transition to which may give rise to severe structural unemployment. Part of the existing capital stock is inflexible in terms of employment generation because it is old vintage and uncompetitive, and hence cannot be transferred to new uses. Attempts to spin out its life by defensive investment and rising capital intensity may only exacerbate the unemployment problem. Furthermore, new technological systems tend to be more capital-intensive than the old requiring less labour per unit of capital. Thus if the transition is delayed, there may be a capital shortage leading to rising unemployment despite surplus capacity of the old vintages. The hiatus in investment in new technology may be caused by a number of factors, for example, a lag in identifying new consumer wants, or the appearance of exogenous shocks which adversely affect expectations about the future.[5]

Essentially these theories are structural and supply-oriented and often they form part of long-wave theories in economic activity and innovation. They stress the importance of real growth forces and the need for continuing structural change, with monetary factors and demand management policies featuring only incidentally. Indeed, Freeman *et al.* and Mensch very much doubt whether conventional demand expansionary policies could 'tilt' the economic system out of a long-term structural recession, at least not without awkward consequences.[6]

The crucial question is how far these theories are relevant to the problems of the recent past. By definition it is difficult to substantiate one way or another the notion of innovational clustering despite heroic attempts by Schumpeter and later writers.[7] In any case we do not propose to get embroiled here in long-wave theories on which much has been written in recent years. However, it is difficult to substantiate Mensch's theory regarding the lack of basic innovations as a cause of the recent slow-down in growth, in view of the important developments in electronics, information research, nuclear power, energy and pharmaceuticals. Certainly, the apparent sudden break in growth after 1973 might be difficult to explain in these terms. On the other hand, despite these reservations a hiatus in investment prospects in the western world can be discerned in the recent past.

To substantiate this point it is necessary to recall briefly the sources of post-war growth. The major industrial nations prospered in the favourable international economic climate of the 1950s and 1960s but the main source of growth was the rapid diffusion of technological backlogs in Europe which resulted in high investment and resource reallocation with a favourable impact on productivity growth and profitability. Manufacturing was the dynamic sector and there was a rapid diffusion of known techniques in energy-intensive sectors including automobiles, electrical products, chemicals and consumer durable goods. This stimulated high levels of investment and encouraged a rapid shift of resources, mainly labour, from low-productivity agriculture to high growth, high-productivity areas in manufacturing. By the middle of the 1970s average productivity levels in many European countries were 80 per cent or more of the American as against an average of 50 per cent in 1950.[8] Thus during this period Europe was able to reduce the productivity gap significantly and by the latter date the scope for substantial gains from moving towards best practice techniques was steadily diminishing. The declining rate of return in manufacturing tends to lend support to the thesis that the limits to technical diffusion were squeezing profitability.

In other words, by the early 1970s the major industrial economies had exhausted much of their growth potential under the existing technological format. In Van Duijn's terminology, the product life-cycles of many leading sectors of the 1950s and 1960s were approaching maturity and additional innovations in these sectors tended increasingly to take the form of labour-saving process innovations. At the same time major employment-creating product innovations in the new rapid growth sectors were less well represented than in the past.[9] Furthermore, the basic infrastructure investment to serve the needs of the leading growth sectors of the previous decade had been over-expanded, giving rise to growing excess capacity in basic industries such as steel, shipbuilding, basic chemicals and construction. Hence some slowing-down in the growth momentum was to be expected by the early 1970s, irrespective of external events, until the transition to a new technological growth profile had been established. The shocks of the 1970s – notably the commodity and oil price explosions and the ensuing inflationary consequences – checked the transition by adversely affecting expectations. Thus profitability deteriorated, defensive cost-cutting (labour-saving) measures were adopted and the exploitation of new techniques was postponed. Not surprisingly, the leading energy-intensive sectors were hit particularly hard by the crisis of the 1970s as were the over-expanded infrastructure industries. The terms of trade of manufactured products deteriorated as real energy prices rose sharply, in contrast to the decline in the two decades to 1972 which had favoured their expansion. The terms of trade of manufacturing industry against a weighted average of oil and non-oil primary product prices worsened by 50 per cent in the two years 1972-4, and though this was eventually reversed through 1975-8, as a result of high inflation in the industrial countries and an easing in the oil market, the second oil price hike at the end of the decade led to a further deterioration in the terms of trade of manufactured products of the order of 40 per cent.[10] Since initially there was limited offset to this decline through increased productivity or downward real wage adjustment the burden was borne by capital in the form of greatly squeezed profits.[11]

It may be argued therefore that the trend towards industrial disequilibrium was apparent before the shocks of the 1970s made matters worse. But the latter simply accelerated the process of maturity in the once former growth industries. In an ideal world, the process of industrial re-orientation or restructuring should have been started in the second half of the 1960s (compare the Edwardian period) when the product life-cycle of many leading industries was approaching maturity, but economic agents, conditioned by the past high growth background, were slow to innovate and identify new consumer needs until it was too late. The oil shocks came at a most inopportune time since they undermined the energy-intensive structure of activity as it was reaching maturity and at the same time impaired the profitability of enterprise. According to Van Duijn, technology *per se* was not the real bottleneck since the technological foundations for new growth industries had already been laid; rather it was the tardy recognition of changing demand structures and subsequently the lack of financial means as a result of the profits squeeze which delayed the transition to a new technological base.[12]

THE TRANSITION THEORY

Technology may not be the only source of secular structural disequilibrium. Beenstock has identified an alternative causal force in his Transition Theory.[13] Here the operative factor is the growing competition from the lesser developed countries (LDCs) which threatens the existing economic structures of the mature industrial economies (MIEs). In Beenstock's own words: 'The surge of LDC industrialisation that began in the mid-1960s triggered a sequence of global economic adjustments in the following fifteen years that has underpinned the protracted recession in the bloc of industrialised countries.'[14] The sequence is as follows: the rapid advance of industrialisation in the LDCs from the later 1960s onwards (and which was scarcely checked in the 1970s) leads to increased competition in the world market for manufactures, and this causes the price of manufactures to fall relative to the price of commodities. Rates of return in manufacturing decline in the MIEs but rise in the LDCs, and resources therefore shift out of manufacturing in the former countries while capital moves from the MIEs to the LDCs whose current account deficits are the counterpart of capital account surpluses which allows them to import capital goods to further their industrialisation drive. As the manufacturing sector in the mature economies contracts and adjusts to the new situation, structural or mismatch unemployment occurs since any structural adjustment takes time to complete and cannot be frictionless in imperfect markets. However, it is only a temporary condition until a new equilibrium structure is achieved, that is, providing a new batch of LDCs do not repeat the process again.[15]

The Beenstock theory contrasts with that of traditional aggregate demand deficiency, though the author does not eschew the influence of the latter entirely. But he argues that the protracted nature of the slow-down is unlikely to have been caused by a permanent deficiency in demand on the grounds that an interval of ten years or so should have been sufficient to restore the balance on this count.[16] In any case the structural break in unemployment occurred well before (1967 onwards) the oil price hikes and inflation of the 1970s, and by 1972 unemployment levels were back to those of the early 1950s. On the other hand, some doubt may be expressed regarding the strength of manufacturing competition of the LDCs in world markets. It is true that their share of world manufacturing output and trade rose steadily after 1965, from 10.4 per cent in 1965 to 15.5 per cent in 1980 in the case of output and 5.1 to 9.8 per cent for the trade share, but in the case of the latter the proportion only increased marginally between 1965-70 (5.1- 5.6 per cent), that is the crucial period as far as the industrial break in the mature economies is concerned. Rothwell and Zegveld, for example, claim that international competition among the major industrial economies was a more important influence than competition from the LDCs.[17]

Though aggregate demand deficiency is not considered to be an important long-term problem, the Transition Theory is recognised as being complementary to other theories of unemployment. Thus the shocks of the 1970s accentuated the trends already apparent, though according to Beenstock, only the level and not the rate of growth of output was permanently affected. Thus in the absence of any shocks output growth (GDP) in the mature economies would have averaged around 4 per cent in the 1970s as against an out-turn of $3\frac{1}{2}$ per cent, and 6 per cent in the previous decade.[18] The impact on manufacturing output was certainly more substantial. Bruno, for example, reckons that the rise in relative import prices accounted for between 40-60 per cent of the decline in OECD manufacturing growth in the 1970s.[19] However, as far as employment is concerned, the disturbances had two important repercussions. Because of the sharp rise in real energy prices (174 per cent for industrial users between 1973 and 1981) the equilibrium real wage level fell, thereby generating classical unemployment until the real wage level adjusted to the new equilibrium level. Adjustment was slow however because of the inflexibility of wages, hence the squeeze on profit margins.[20] Secondly, the rise in oil prices rendered a large proportion of the existing capital stock obsolete; Beenstock estimates that about one-third of the pre-oil price rise capital stock became obsolete and consequently subsequent measures of capacity utilisation severely understate the degree of capital utilisation. The impact would of course be felt in terms of a severe employment capital shortage (see below).

JOBLESS GROWTH

A wider structural interpretation of the current unemployment crisis has been presented by Rothwell and Zegveld.[21] They also argue that the decline in manufacturing employment cannot be attributed simply to lower growth and the weakness of demand; in fact, rather the reverse causal sequence, that lower growth and rising unemployment are a function of structural and technical changes which, they feel, will persist and intensify in the 1980s. A pattern of jobless growth in manufacturing became established in the later 1960s due to pronounced long-term structural changes in patterns of economic activity. The identify several causal factors, including shifting patterns of consumer demand, the decline in the rate at which new products come onto the market, a growing mismatch between skills and employment needs, shifts in production and hence employment to low wage cost developing countries and changes in production technology and techniques. But primary emphasis is placed on the employment effects of technical change which manifests itself in several different ways though the final consequences are always the same: job losses and skill reorientation. Thus the competition from low labour cost producers of the Third World intensifies price competition in traditional industries, such as textiles, shipbuilding, car manufacturing and light engineering, which displaces jobs in the mature economies and encourages the adoption of cost-cutting (labour saving) techniques, thereby creating further job displacement.

However, more important, according to the authors, has been the increased competition among the advanced industrial countries in sophisticated products which has induced the search for labour-saving techniques, the full impact of which began to be felt from the mid-1960s, together with the long-term impact of continuous 'clay-clay' technical change, that is, incremental labour-saving technical change which is continuously embodied in successive vintages of equipment resulting in a steady decline in employment opportunities as labour efficiency improves through greater capital intensity. A third feature they identify is the secular trend towards greater capital intensity of production as a response to the shift in relative factor prices and falling profit margins. The labour: capital price ratio deteriorated in most European countries from the mid-1950s and the adverse shift was considerably intensified by generous tax-based investment incentives, especially in Britain, which kept down the cost of capital relative to labour,[22] and from the later 1960s by high wage inflation, rising social security payments and job protection and compensation legislation. This had a two-fold effect. Firms became less inclined to regard labour as a variable cost and were therefore more cautious about hiring additional labour, while the trend towards labour-saving (capital-intensive) investment was accentuated, which took the form of a rationalisation of existing production facilities rather than extensive new capacity creation.[23]

Using data drawn from a study by Cox (1978), Rothwell and Zegveld demonstrate the pressures which force firms to shed labour and substitute rationalisation investment for growth investment. As can be seen from Table 4.1, employment in the UK and German mechanical engineering industries declined when a mismatch occurred between the growth in sales receipts and that in employment costs even though output in real terms was still rising. Quoting Cox,

in current output technological development is responsible for maintaining and increasing sales and, potentially, the numbers employed. If, however, unions negotiate an average cost per employee that is out of line with increase in sales receipts, then technical development comes to play an additional role – that of substituting machine effort for human effort, which has become too expensive.[24]

TABLE 4.1: **Rise in Value of Sales Receipts, Costs per Employee and Employment Changes in Mechanical Engineering in the UK and West Germany**

	Costs per Employee	*Sales*	*Change in Employment*
	(per cent per annum)		
UK			
1958-63	3	6	+56,000
1963-67	7	9	+33,000
1967-71	12	14	+54,000
1971-75	23	19	-73,000
West Germany			
1967-71	15	16	+143,900
1971-75	9	7	-96,000

Source: Rothwell and Zegweld, *op. cit.*, p.50, note 1.

As a consequence of the above factors, a pattern of jobless growth became firmly established in the later 1960s, a trend which was intensified in the 1970s as high wage inflation and declining profit margins made imperative the adoption of labour-saving investment and rationalisation of production facilities. The extension of new growth capacity was neglected, thereby giving rise to capital shortage unemployment despite the existence of much excess and obsolete capacity.

However, it should be noted that it is not simply traditional industries subject to severe competitive and/or wage cost pressures which have suffered labour displacement. Rapid technical change, as a result of the beginnings of the electronic revolution, is starting to have a significant impact on old and new industries alike. Watchmaking, for example, has been transformed overnight in terms of its product structure and the labour displaced from the old mechanical operations (e.g. Timex in Scotland) will never be re-absorbed in the same capacity again. What is even more significant is that the high growth electronics industry itself has shifted rapidly from being a labour-intensive industry in the 1950s to a highly capital-intensive jobless growth sector by the 1970s. The main cause has been the large productivity gains as a result of rapid technical change of which the latest stage is microelectronics. Thus in the United States total employment in the electronics production industry rose from 56,000 in 1939 to 350,000 in 1950; subsequently there was a further rapid rise to a peak of 1.254 million in 1969 after which employment declined gradually. Employment growth in the European electronics industry has now levelled off and in some sectors of the industry employment is falling rapidly. The telecommunications industry provides a striking example, though microelectronics has still to make its major impact on telecommunications — which will radically alter the manpower requirements of both the user and producer industries – the telecommunications production industry experienced a sharp drop in employment during the 1970s as the old electro-mechanical Strowger production was replaced by the first generation electronic equipment TXE4. Thus employment in Britain's telecommunications industry fell by nearly one-third in the 1970s despite a large increase in the volume of output.

The impact at the micro-level can be seen from the data for Standard Telephones and Cables, one of the main British producers (Table 4.2). Between 1974 and 1982 the workforce declined by 35 per cent on the back of a substantial rise in the company's output. This sharp drop was occasioned by the rapid phasing out of the old electro-mechanical switchgear during the 1970s together with a big increase in capital investment per employee as the switch to new generation equipment proceeded.[25] The result was not only a dramatic shift in the ratio of material to labour and overhead costs – the 30:70 ratio of 1970 was more or less reversed by 1980 under the new electronic technology – but it also meant redundancy for many older workers and a vast retraining programme involving some 7000 workers. It is the latter aspect of the mismatch problem which is most important in the long run and which requires careful planning. It is not simply a numbers game since, as Peter Young has noted, it was a much more complex situation than getting a job in the 1930s had been: 'For many employees at all levels it meant coming to terms with themselves, submitting to being assessed, having to go to school again, moving to a new job in a new community, readjusting status and expectations as one competed with younger people in new skills like programming, even establishing a new identity.'[26] Similarly, the next generation of equipment – the fully electronic System X or variants thereof – is likely to lead to a further drop in numbers engaged in telecommunications production and skill re-orientation since one unit of equipment can be produced by one-tenth the labour force required for the TXE4.

TABLE 4.2: **Sales and Employment of Standard Telephones and Cables, 1974-82**

	1974	*1976*	*1978*	*1980*	*1982*
Sales (£ m)	241.8	315.3	373.6	537.7	628.5
Average no. of UK employees (000s)	35.2	31.6	28.0	27.3	22.9

Source: Standard Telephones and Cables, *Annual Report*, 1982.

The full impact of the microelectronics revolution throughout industry is likely to intensify the trend towards jobless growth in the future, though one should take care not to exaggerate the net labour displacement effect, as Beenstock cautions,[27] since in the past all new technologies have created new jobs as well as destroying old ones. However, it is very unlikely that the manufacturing sector will resume its role as an important employment generator as in the past. Much will depend therefore on whether new jobs can be created in the services sector which in the 1970s was an important source of employment opportunities, though latterly employment prospects here have dwindled markedly. For several reasons the outlook is none too promising. First, public sector employment, formerly a very buoyant area, is likely to remain flat given the constraints on public spending, though this of course could change with a shift in political opinion. Second, the pressure for wage parity in service occupations, many of which are highly labour-intensive and have low productivity and capital-intensive levels, will generate pressures to rationalise operations and introduce labour-saving investment. Thirdly, the scope for improvements in productivity through the introduction of electronic equipment is considerable in many service trades such as banking, insurance and office work, and this will eventually cause a loss of jobs. It is true that new jobs and activities will be created by the diffusion of microelectronics, but it seems unlikely that this will lead to a renewed explosion of service employment on the scale of the past.

Whatever importance we attach to the conflicting claims regarding structural disequilibrium, there seems little doubt that the rise in unemployment in the western economies in the last decade and a half cannot be attributed solely to a deficiency of aggregate demand. If this were the case the solution to its correction would be less problematic. However, the evidence suggests that there were fundamental long-term forces at work creating tensions within the advanced industrial countries and giving rise to heavy structural unemployment and mismatch employment opportunities which are difficult to cure by conventional means. These forces were in turn exacerbated by the shocks of the 1970s. Before discussing the policy implications, we must consider briefly why Britain's unemployment problem was more severe than that of other countries.

BRITAIN'S PAROCHIAL PROBLEMS

Though the deceleration in Britain's total output growth in the 1970s was not out of line with that of her major competitors, the downward break in the industrial sector started earlier and was greater than elsewhere. The proportionate decline in manufacturing activity through to the early 1980s exceeded that of the major industrial countries and in 1980 manufacturing's share of non-oil output was back to the 1948 level at one of the lowest among the industrial countries. As we have seen, it is this sector which accounts for the bulk of the employment losses since the second half of the 1960s, so that it is not surprising that Britain's unemployment has been unusually intense.

While the onset of deindustrialisation and restructuring may be written in global terms, the disparity between Britain and her major trading partners requires an indigenous explanation. Two factors are mainly responsible for the relative deterioration: first, the accumulated effect of the declining competitiveness of Britain's industry, and second, the structural impact of becoming an oil producer. Additionally, short-term policy measures may have accentuated the decline in recent years, though it is unclear whether macro-policies have been that much more severe than elsewhere in the western world.[28]

The first factor is a long-standing issue and one that has been well aired in the literature. While there may be some debate as to the long-term origins of Britain's relative decline, for the present purposes we need go no further back than 1950. At that time British industry was in a relatively strong position with a level of output per head not too dissimilar from that of her main competitors other than the United States. Exports had risen sharply in the later 1940s, admittedly in a favourable selling environment, and the devaluation of sterling in 1949 gave an additional boost to competitiveness. Despite this initial advantage British industry's competitive position began to deteriorate soon after and, apart from temporary fluctuations, has continued to do so at an accelerating rate through to the present. The key factor in the situation has been the very weak performance in productivity. Between 1950 and 1978 the rate of growth of output per person employed in industry was only about half that of other industrial nations including the United States, which incidentally also had a poor record. Thus by the end of the period productivity levels in Britain across a broad spectrum of the economy, and particularly in industry, were well below those of her main competitors.[29] The low productivity growth can be attributed to several interrelated factors, including a slow rate of technical innovation, poor utilisation of capital stock, low investment, limited structural adaptation to take full opportunity of rapid growth sectors, and severe overmanning throughout industry, the latter partly a function of the previously listed factors.[30] Estimates for overmanning in the 1960s vary from between 20-30 per cent of the numbers employed in British industry, and possibly up to 5 million persons could have been released from production work had concealed unemployment been eliminated.[31]

At the same time price and exchange movements have worked against British industry intermittently. Though UK price inflation was not out of line with that of other countries through to the mid-1960s, the real value of the exchange rate rose by 21 per cent between the 1949 and 1967 devaluations, and the devaluation in the latter year did not fully restore the relative competitive position prevailing after the 1949 devaluation. Thus by the mid-1960s the UK was losing ground both in terms of price and labour cost competitiveness. The 1967 devaluation and the subsequent depreciation of sterling after it was floated in 1972 helped to rectify the position, and despite higher domestic inflation price and labour cost competitiveness improved through to 1976/7, more especially after 1972. Subsequently the position deteriorated again with sterling appreciating strongly on account of Britain becoming an oil producer, and at a time when domestic inflation was higher than elsewhere.[32] In recent years there has been some relief from the fall in sterling and a lower rate of domestic inflation together with a sharp uplift in productivity.

However, as Singh has noted,[33] price competitiveness is not the sole determinant of Britain's trading performance since in the decade or so through to the middle of the 1970s, when the price trends were on balance moving favourably, the trading record of manufacturing continued to deteriorate due to unfavourable demand elasticities which made it difficult to meet foreign competition in either home or overseas markets.[34] Even more significant is the fact that Britain's share of world trade held up rather better in the later 1970s when the exchange rate and unit labour costs moved against her. This would imply that non-price factors are at the root of Britain's weak trading performance, for example, low quality of products, poor design, bad marketing, slack delivery schedules and inadequate after-sales service. On the export front such weaknesses are reflected in the low unit price that Britain receives for her manufactured exports, indicating that technically inferior products sink to the bottom end of the price range.[35] The main problem is not so much that the structural mix of exports is wrong but rather the general inefficiency and slow technical progress in manufacturing which makes it difficult to sell products, and it is significant that those industries and sectors with rapid productivity growth are better able to remain internationally competitive.[36]

The signs of Britain's underlying competitive weakness, whatever its ultimate causes, are visible for all to see. Britain's share of world exports of manufactures fell from 25.3 per cent in 1950 to less than 9 per cent in the mid-1970s, after which there was a slight recovery. Conversely, imports of manufactures now account for some two-thirds of all imports, compared with 20 per cent in the early 1950s, while the import penetration ratio (imports/domestic demand + exports) increased from around 6 per cent in the later 1950s to over 20 per cent by the end of the 1970s.[37] As the figures in Table 4.3 indicate, imports of manufactures have consistently risen faster than either domestic output or exports of manufactures while they have also exceeded the overall rate of growth in world trade.

TABLE 4.3: **Average Annual Growth Rates of UK Output, Exports and Imports of Manufactures, 1957-77**

	1957-67	*1967-77*
Output	2.8	1.4
Imports	9.4	9.0
Exports	2.7	6.7
World Trade	7.7	8.3

Source: F. Blackaby (ed.), *De-industrialisation* (1979), p. 23.

An indication of the impact of import penetration on manufacturing has been given by Eltis, who estimates that by

1974 UK manufacturing output would have been 24 per cent higher than it actually was had imports of manufactures risen over the previous decade at the same rate as that of GDP.[38] Perhaps even more illustrative in this context are the examples of decline of once flourishing sectors of British industry largly as the result of general inefficiency and neglect of innovation. Two examples must suffice, though many more could be quoted. The first one is the textile machinery industry in which Britain once reigned supreme, and even as late as 1954 her share of world trade in textile machinery was 30 per cent. Subsequently the industry has almost collapsed in this country; by 1975 Britain's share of the world market was down to 11 per cent, whereas Germany's share over the same period had risen from 18 to 35 per cent, while employment was decimated from 75,000 to 35,000. To all intents and purposes the main reason for the setback was the failure to exploit the technical changes required to maintain international competitiveness, partly through neglect of R & D and limited recruitment of technical skills.[39]

The machine tool industry shared a somewhat similar fate. Despite considerable government financial assistance in the decade or so through to the end of the 1970s, Britain fared very badly in this field. By 1979 output was 22 per cent down on 1968 and one-third below the peak year of 1970, as against increases of 22 per cent in the United States and 10 per cent in Germany over the same period. Employment fell by over 20 per cent (1968-78), export volume by 18 per cent, while imports accounted for 47 per cent of the home market in 1979 compared with 28 per cent in 1970 and Britain's share of world exports declined from 13 to 6 per cent between 1965-78. Again it was a neglect of innovation and R & D expenditure, which fell dramatically in the 1970s, together with a failure to capitalise on the initial advantage in numerically-controlled machine tools, which were largely responsible for the disappointing performance of this industry.[40]

However, the problem is more than simply one of failing to introduce new products based on new technology. In some branches of industry the whole structure of production is antiquated and requires complete scrapping and redesigning to meet contemporary needs. The engineering industry in general, and mechanical engineering especially, provides a classic example, though not the only one, in which the plant, its lay-out, design and work practices are obsolete, such that a fairly typical picture of the day-to-day operations in a British engineering factory has been described by a leading consulting engineer as follows:

Fork trucks hauling materials everywhere, damaging and losing parts; progress chasers and half the supervisory staff trying to find parts for their next operation; operators going for tools while their machines sit idle; aisles full of people dodging the fork trucks; complex production control systems trying to keep track of thousands of transactions each day; inspectors trying to separate bad parts from good throughout the process; late deliveries; delivery lead time measured in months for products with a routed manufacturing time measured in a few hours.

If most manufacturing systems were designed from scratch for today's products, volumes, product mixes and new technology, the new plants 'would not remotely resemble the present operation.'[41]

In other words, because of accumulating inefficiency and lags in moving towards best practice techniques British industry had more to lose in the way of excess and obsolete capacity, both capital and labour, than her competitors when economic conditions deteriorated in the 1970s. Thus Britain's structural problem, as in the 1920s, is much greater than that of many other countries, and it is not therefore surprising that the labour shake-out in manufacturing has been that much the greater. To complicate matters, Britain was becoming an oil producer at this time which imposed a further structural readjustment on the economy.

STRUCTURAL IMPACT OF OIL PRODUCTION

Initially Britain was badly hit by the first oil price rise and energy scare because of her dependence on imported oil. Shortly afterwards indigenous oil began to come on stream and by the early 1980s Britain was self-sufficient in oil, the production of which accounted for around 6 per cent of GDP. This eventually relieved the balance of payments, but it also

meant that Britain was exposed to greater structural adjustment than non-oil producing OECD countries in order to
make way for oil production. Since oil production improves
the balance of payments and for a time the exchange rate, the
sector to suffer is that in non-oil traded goods. As Beenstock
has demonstrated, the oil trade 'crowds out' the non-oil trade
in the balance of payments since, as the exchange rate rises,
imports increase and exports are checked.[42] In this way the
country benefits through the terms of trade effect and
consumption and real income are higher than they would
otherwise have been. However, in the process the largest
trading sector, manufacturing, bears the brunt of the burden of
adjustment. Since Britain has become an oil producer non-oil
imports have risen much faster than exports, the latter lagging
the growth in world trade, while the non-oil balance has
deteriorated *pari passu* with the improvement in the oil
balance. Thus while the possession of oil confers considerable
benefits it does affect adversely the structure of manufacturing
activity which is very exposed to external trade. Employment
falls rapidly and cannot be matched by comparable opportunities in the capital-intensive oil production sector. As we have
seen, much of the increase in unemployment has occurred in
manufacturing, as opposed to the sheltered service trades,
and the influence of oil production has made a substantial
contribution to mismatch unemployment in manufacturing.
By the early 1980s the main structural impact of oil was
complete, since Britain was by that time self-sufficient in oil,
while the upward pressure on sterling was relieved by the slack
conditions in the world oil market.

FISCAL REFLATION AND STRUCTURAL ADJUSTMENT

During the last fifteen years or so the major industrial
economies, including the British, have been subject to increasing structural strains which have given rise to severe mismatch
unemployment. These problems have been aggravated by
exogenous shocks, policy reactions to the impact of the
shocks, and general demand deficiency. It is argued that
structural or disequilibrium unemployment is both large and

long-term in nature and that conventional policies of demand management are not appropriate to deal with the problem. Indeed a large-scale expansionary stimulus designed to produce a quick effect on the unemployment level could in fact backfire and ultimately lead to a worsened employment situation.

The reasoning behind this conclusion is twofold. First, a conventional policy approach of the magnitude required would run up against the economic and financial constraints specified in Chaper 3, and also create a renewed inflationary problem (Chapter 6). The end result would therefore be a further bout of policy retrenchment to appease financial markets. The recent policy reversals in France demonstrate the limits to government measures which damage the financial framework of society. The consequences would be as before: a further squeeze on profits, declining investment and output and reduced employment prospects, with unemployment probably rising to a higher level than at the previous peak. The effects of another policy shift would clearly not provide the right climate to foster structural change, which brings us to the second main point in the argument: that reflationary policies of any substantial scale would do little directly to promote structural adjustment; in fact they may well retard it and thereby weaken the long-term viability of the economy. Before looking at points of detail in the latter context, it is useful to comment on why there is a need for structural change.

When structural disequilibrium and structural unemployment are endemic it is normally the case that the disequilibrium arises as a result of a failure to adjust the pattern of economic activity to shifting demand-and-supply conditions. The origins of the structural problem may be of a long-term and partly indigenous nature, as in the case of Britain, where the ability of the economy to adapt over time has been limited for one reason or another. Alternatively, and/or additionally, more general pressures for adjustment may derive from secular forces or external shocks of the type experienced since the mid-1960s which have threatened or at least strained the economic base of many western economies. Both processes have been at work with particular force in Britain.

The important point at this stage is not the causal sequence of structural imbalance which has already been specified, but the necessity for adaptation. Put simply, if structural imbalance is primarily a product of a failure to adjust, then there can be no satisfactory long-term alternative to a policy of adjustment. The consequences of not doing so are readily specified and are applicable equally at the macro- and micro-levels: the product mix becomes distorted, the technological base weakens and the capital:labour ratio becomes unbalanced. The end result is declining competitiveness, loss of market shares and the inevitable consequences for capital and labour markets arising therefrom.

The real issue however is not simply that of perceiving the need for transformation, which at some stage presumably becomes all too obvious, but rather the difficulty of finding ways to deal with the problem. In a utopian or ideal market situation, where resources are perfectly mobile and transferable and with an absence of rigidities in capital and labour markets, there would be little difficulty since resources would reallocate themselves quickly and thereby the degree of mismatch would be minimised. But unfortunately conditions in the real world are very different. Factors of production are both lumpy and heterogeneous and therefore cannot readily be transferred to alternative activities. Thus redundant capacity in shipbuilding cannot be converted to the production of pharmaceuticals however perfect might be the second-hand market in capital goods, while unemployed steel workers cannot be transformed into microelectronics technicians, at least not without a considerable amount of retraining. Other impediments to transfer may arise because of restrictive practices on the part of labour or defensive action by management, as well as social factors relevant to mobility (see Chapter 5).

Such impediments inevitably mean that structural adjustment cannot be achieved quickly. It follows therefore that when capacity destruction (both in capital and labour markets) becomes endemic the resource mismatch problem is both large and of long duration. Moreover, it can give rise to what may at first sight seem a puzzling dichotomy, namely that of scarcity amid plenty: that is in certain regions and industries there may be plenty of spare capacity and labour while in others there is a shortage of both, a situation which reflects not simply the lack of homogeneity among factors of production, and hence their non-transferability to other uses, but also to the fact that redundant resources may be obsolete in any context. If capital obsolescence is a major problem then an economy-wide capital shortage may arise until new capacity comes on stream. The destruction of old capacity and the creation of new is however an essential part of the required technological transformation in conditions of structural disequilibrium.

Turning to the British context, the main structural priorities may be specified as follows: (1) the need to shift resources from low-productivity, ex-growth sectors to high-growth, technologically advanced industries; (2) to ensure that more resources are converted into exchange earnings either through import-saving or increased exports or both; and (3) that a high rate of technological innovation and efficiency is maintained throughout the economy. If these objectives can be achieved, then Britain's growth prospects would improve and so too would those of employment.

Given the present high level of unemployment, any reflationary package would almost certainly be geared towards employment generation, and so the package would be designed to secure the maximum benefit on this count. One would anticipate therefore that priority would be given to labour-intensive activities including public works such as roads and construction, public service employment generally, assistance to labour-intensive declining industries, together with some increase in transfer payments and income redistribution through the tax system which would raise the level of aggregate demand.

This macro-policy orientation can be criticised on several counts bearing in mind the critical structural priorities listed above. The overall effect would be to freeze the *status quo* and thereby retard structural transformation.

(1) In conditions of severe structural disequilibrium it is essential that the opportunity be taken to scrap obsolete and inefficient plant in declining sectors and redirect resources into expanding areas and new technologies. Freeman *et al.* refer to the process as one of creative capacity destruction.[43] However,

a boost to demand through fiscal action will tend to strengthen resistance to the elimination of old marginal plant which becomes increasingly uncompetitive and therefore acts as a drag on the economy. Similarly, direct support for ailing or 'lamc-duck' industries or enterprises on employment grounds (though there have been a few notable high technology exceptions) will simply prolong or spin out the adjustment process and reduce the overall level of efficiency. Provided capital markets are reasonably efficient, such forms of assistance tend to waste resources and increase the resistance to economic change since the virtual absence of market signals leads to a misallocation of resources.

Such observations are not intended to decry the utility of an industrial and/or technological policy specifically designed to improve Britain's industrial structure. Unfortunately, the record on this score over the past two decades has not been a happy one. Despite a massive amount of government intervention and assistance at the micro-level there is very little to show for it. In general governments have been strong on baling out losers, but have had a bad track record when it comes to picking winners.[44] They have spent large sums to support declining industries in order to protect employment, but relatively little on new growth industries (excepting aerospace and nuclear power), or on fostering the process of technological and structural change. Subsidies have been one of Britain's few growth industries, and, as Maunder observes, no one most of the time has had the faintest idea how they are supposed to work, what they are intended to achieve and whether they have had any effect except for propping up relatively inefficient sectors and employment.[45] In time a prolonged and substantial programme of support for these sectors could seriously reduce the resources available for the potential growth areas of the economy. The general consensus seems to be that industrial policies as conceived in this country have significantly retarded the progress of industrial and structural change and thereby reduced the efficiency with which resouces are deployed.[46] Britain's record in this respect contrasts sharply with that of Japan where, despite a much smaller public sector, the nature and quality of government intervention and assistance has been vastly superior in that it

85

has concentrated on giving incentives to firms adopting new technology and introducing productivity-raising innovations while refusing to bolster up failures.[47]

(2) Similar arguments apply to labour; it is equally important to 'scrap' human capital though in this case the problem is more difficult because of the social issues involved. However, redeployment is a crucial feature of structural transformation; it is essential to release workers from old, declining, low-productivity sectors where attitudes and skills are inimical to progress, and wherever possible to retrain redundant workers with new skills to equip them for the new technological age. Simply because unemployment is currently high is no excuse for slowing down the process of change since in the long run it would merely reduce the competitiveness of individual industries and the economy as a whole. It follows therefore that policy orientation should be towards manpower planning and retraining programmes rather than policies which bolster the employment prospects of sectors with no long-term future.

(3) A reflationary macro-economic policy will tend to be directed towards sectors which require relatively limited amounts of new capital but which generate a good deal of employment. These would include not only traditional public works activities such as roads and construction of one form or another, but also public services in general which have been one of the largest absorbers of labour in the last fifteen years or so. This approach would have several disadvantages. First, it would induce a shift of resources into low-productivity, low-technology sectors which is the opposite of what is required. Secondly, public sector activities, with a few exceptions, generate few exports and offer little scope for import saving so that the resource shift would be detrimental to the balance of payments. Moreover, some of the additional incomes generated by raising the employment level in the public sector would leak into imports, thereby further eroding the strength of the external account. A further possibility is that a large increase in spending on public services could lead to some financial crowding out of the private sector, though the extent of this would depend upon the size of the fiscal thrust and the response of financial markets to it (see Chapter 3). Hawkins

has outlined the disadvantages of public sector employment generation in the following terms:

> But this form of job creation is ultimately tax-dependent and as such implies a growing squeeze on the incomes of those in self-financing employment. The implications of such a squeeze for inflation, the balance of payments and the capacity of the industrial and private sector to generate more wealth would hardly be consistent with a strategy aimed at reducing the level of unemployment.[48]

(4) General reflation aimed specifically at reducing unemployment would do little to promote technological change, nor would it enhance the overall level of efficiency. Indeed, from what has already been said, the probability is that the efficiency of resource use would decline. Hence there would be no improvement in competitiveness or the structural properties of the traded goods sector. Moreover, expansionary policies might strengthen labour market rigidities – trade union attitudes and practices – which Maynard believes have greatly increased the difficulty of operating a successful macroeconomic policy. In these circumstances, any return to previous policies 'would seem likely to condemn the UK to remaining a low productivity, high inflation economy without providing any guarantee at all that high levels of employment could be maintained'.[49]

(5) The inflationary implications relevant to the present context are worth emphasising. (Inflation is discussed more fully in Chapter 6.) Generally these would be adverse. In a structurally-weak situation the price effects of reflation would come through more strongly than the output effects. This may partly reflect the existence of real wage rigidity, but more likely it would signify the emergence of supply bottlenecks arising from a prolonged period of capital obsolescence and the properties of technical change. Following a lengthy period of slack growth, capital obsolescence and technical change with a labour-saving bias, the existing capital stock may be insufficient to generate full employment. Britain, moreover, has long suffered from the disadvantage of having a low level of capital equipment per worker compared with her major trading competitors. Cooper and Clark have described such conditions as an 'undercapitalisation trap'

in which attempts to increase fixed investment by demand expansion are doomed to be short-term and ineffective, owing to the need to reverse such policies in the face of inflation and/or balance of payments problems arising from the inability of the supply side of the economy, with its low level of productive capacity, to respond.

In other words, given an expansionary stimulus the existing capital stock becomes fully utilised before full employment is reached and the main response is inflationary. Further attempts to stimulate employment only exacerbate the inflationary pressures and eventually lead to policy retrenchment.[50]

Clearly this has all the characteristics of a vicious circle. Additional capacity is required to create more output and employment, but attempts to generate it are frustrated by the original capacity bottleneck so that the economic constraints come into play. If these dictate a reversal of expansionary policies then investment expectations will be dampened once again with little prospect of relieving the capacity bottleneck. But even assuming this is not the case, the prospects for strong expansion may be limited. Higher inflation and the possibility of renewed deterioration in the real product wage would serve to depress business confidence and investment plans, or at best it would stimulate further labour-saving technology, all of which would weaken employment opportunities. Furthermore, after a prolonged period of depressed demand, the supply capability of the capital goods sector may be limited with the result that any sharp boost in demand for investment goods would raise their product prices and thereby cause some firms to postpone investment. The moral of this exercise therefore is that in a structurally-weak situation it is not possible to produce a quick and viable capacity and employment response by conventional means. The economic system is relatively inflexible in the short term, and any attempt to force it unduly can be no more successful than pushing on a piece of string.

As conventionally conceived, therefore, a general reflationary package would on balance tend to retard rather than encourage the process of structural change. The structural transformation objectives enumerated above would not be achieved and this would mean a continued deterioration in the viability of the economy and a lowering of employment prospects. In particular, reflation would do little to solve the weaknesses of manufacturing industry; and nor, for that matter, will the present government's policies do much to eliminate non-price competitiveness since 'disciplining the working-class through mass unemployment will not solve a problem of non-price competitiveness even if it does make British manufactures more price and cost competitive.'[51] Yet until something is done to improve the trading performance of manufacturing there can be little prospect of a sustained rise in output and employment. The former large surplus on the manufacturing trading account has been steadily eroded so that, despite the blessing of North Sea oil, the full employment current account would, with our current trading elasticities, be in substantial deficit.[52] Thus, until these improve there can be no question of implementing a full employment package without running into the constraints discussed in Chapter 3. At the risk of repetition, the problem may be emphasised again in the words of the authors of a recent work on the state of British manufacturing:

If the national manufacturing sector is weak, the economy may have to be constrained below full employment since attempts to stimulate domestic activity will draw in manufactured imports and cause a balance of payments crisis. Continuous depreciation of the currency might in the short run stabilise the payments situation, but only at the expense of unacceptable consequences for domestic inflation as imports become continuously more expensive. No orthodox policy instrument will shift the external constraints which are likely to be established by a relatively unsuccessful manufacturing sector. And, outside Cambridge, there is no academic consensus that import controls will work.[53]

If the conclusions sound somewhat less than positive it should be stressed once again that the principle aim of this essay is to demonstrate the constraints to full employment rather than that of providing a solution to the unemployment problem. However, the reader may find a more constructive approach in the concluding chapter of this volume.

The discussion on structural issues has focused primarily on the current situation, though many of the points raised do have relevance to the inter-war years. It would be tedious to repeat the exercise, and in any case some of the inter-war structural aspects are discussed in a regional context in the following chapter.

NOTES

1 J. Cornwall, *Modern Capitalism* (1977); A. Maddison, *Phases of Capitalist Development* (1983); W. W. Rostow, *Why the Poor Get Richer and the Rich Slow Down: Essays in the Marshallian Long Period* (1980).
2 R. Rothwell and W. Zegveld, *Technical Change and Employment* (1979), p.18. With productivity rising faster than output in the latter period.
3 G. Mensch, *Stalemate in Technology: Innovations Overcome Depression* (1979).
4 O. Giarini and H. Loubergé, *The Diminishing Returns of Technology: An Essay on the Crisis in Economic Growth* (1978).
5 C. Freeman, J. Clark and L. Soete, *Unemployment and Technical Innovation: A Study of Long Waves in Economic Development* (1982).
6 Ibid., p.191; Mensch, *op. cit.,* p.32.
7 J. A. Schumpeter, *Business Cycles*, 2 vols (1939).
8 A. Maddison, 'Long-run Dynamics of Productivity Growth', *Banca Nazionale del Lavoro Quarterly Review*, **128** (March 1979).
9 J. J. Van Duijn, *The Long Wave in Economic Life* (1983), pp.138, 207; see also W. W. Rostow, *The World Economy in History* (1978), p.286.
10 Data from G. Maynard, 'Why Oil Prices Must Fall More', *Financial Times*, 23 February 1983.
11 For a more detailed analysis of the repercussions arising from inflation, see Chapter 6.
12 Van Duijn, *op. cit.*, p. 207; see also below.
13 M. Beenstock, *The World Economy in Transition* (1983). This book deserves attention since it dispels many of the myths about current economic problems.
14 Ibid., p.97
15 Ibid., pp.14 – 17.
16 This is not an entirely convincing explanation. Other writers, however, have questioned the demand deficiency explanation. Maynard, for example, argues that 'the attempt to explain Britain's growing unemployment problem through the 1970s in terms of demand deficiency seems difficult to substantiate in view of the fact that in the course of the decade, nominal final expenditure on goods and services rose fourfold. The combination of rising unemployment and balance of payments

deficits, despite a depreciating exchange rate, suggests that the under-pricing of capital and the overpricing of labour was a more pertinent cause.' The steep rise in unemployment in the early 1980s was occasioned to a large extent by the rise in the real exchange rate which had an adverse effect on the real wage rate and profits (see Chapter 6). G. Maynard, 'Microeconomic Deficiencies in UK Macro-economic Policy', *Lloyds Bank Review*, **145** (July 1982), pp.9, 12.

17 Rothwell and Zegveld, *op cit*., p.24.
18 Beenstock, *op. cit.*, p.189.
19 M. Bruno, 'Import Prices and Stagflation in the Industrial Countries: A Cross-sectional Analysis', *Economic Journdl*, **90** (1980); estimates of the impact of oil prices on output vary considerably, with some being quite low. See W. D. Nordhaus, 'Oil and Economic Performance in Industrial Countries', *Brookings Papers on Economic Activity*, 1980 – 1: and J. Tobin, 'Stabilisation Policy Ten Years After', *Brookings Papers on Economic Activity*, 1980-1.
20 Inflation and the real wage level are discussed more fully in Chapter 6.
21 Rothwell and Zegveld, *op cit.*
22 See G. Maynard, 'Microeconomic Deficiences in UK Macroeconomic Policy', *Lloyds Bank Review*, **145** (July 1982), p.7.
23 Cf. M. Scott, *Can We Get Back to Full Employment?* (1978), pp.48, 57 – 64.
24 Rothwell and Zegveld, *op. cit.*, pp.50 – 51, note 1.
25 In ten years capital investment per employee rose eightfold: P. Young, *Power of Speech: A History of Standard Telephones and Cables, 1883* – 1983 (1983), p.181.
26 Young, *op. cit.*, pp.17 – 22, 187 – 8.
27 Beenstock, *op. cit.*, pp.23 – 5, largely in response to the high dis-placement effects postulated by I. Barron and R. Curnow, *The Future of Microelectronics* (1979).
28 It should be recognised of course that restrictive macro-policy may be in part a function of structural weakness.
29 Maddison, *Phases of Capitalist Development*, pp.98, 117 – 18.
30 There is a vast literature on British industry's inefficiency; see in particular C. F. Pratten, 'The Efficiency of British Industry', *Lloyds Bank Review*, **123** (January 1977); and *Labour Productivity Differentials within International Companies* (1976): also A. Cairncross, J. A. Kay and A. Silberston, 'The Regeneration of Manufacturing Industry', *Midland Bank Review* (Autumn 1977).
31 F. Broadway, *State Intervention in British Industry, 1964-68* (1969), p.85.
32 Beenstock, *op. cit.*, p.204: W. E. Martin (ed.), *The Economics of the Profits Crisis* (1981), pp.62 – 3.
33 A. Singh, 'UK Industry and the World Economy: A Case of De-industrialisation', *Cambridge Journal of Economics*, **1** (1977).
34 The most worrying aspect is the high income elasticity of demand for manufactured imports. Most industrial countries have high elasticities but for every 1 per cent increase in national income Britain's imports

of manufactures rise by around 3 per cent compared with just over 2 per cent in the case of Germany and France.

35 See D. K. Stout, *International Price Competitiveness: Non-Price Factors and Export Performance (1977)* and D. Connell, *The UK's performance in Export Markets: Some Evidence from International Trade Data*, (1979).

36 R. Wragg and J. Robertson, 'Britain's Industrial Performance since the War', *Department of Employment Gazette* (May 1978). It would be instructive to have some comparative studies of the export performance of major firms, in particular BTR and Hanson Trust, two of Britain's most successful industrial conglomerates, to see how well they stand up to a trading test. One suspects that foreign bases of manufacture are becoming more attractive than direct exports from the UK which of course reduces the net receipts available to the balance of payments.

37 Over the same period imports of manufactures as a percentage of domestic demand rose from 7 – 8 per cent to 29 per cent. C. J. F. Brown and T. D. Sheriff, 'De-industrialisation: A Background Paper', in F. Blackaby (ed.), *De-industrialisation* (1979), p.244.

38 W. Eltis, in F. Blackaby (ed.), *De-industrialisation* (1979), pp.227-8.

39 Rothwell and Zegveld, *op. cit.*, p.79 – 83.

40 A. Daly, 'Government Support for Innovation in the British Machine Tool Industry: A Case Study', in C. Carter (ed.) *Industrial Policy and Innovation* (1981), pp.60 – 4.

41 P. Bruce, 'Five Point Revival Plan for Engineering Industry', *Financial Times*, 28 April 1983, quoting Brian Small, a leading consulting engineer and joint managing director of Ingersoll, delivering the James Clayton lecture to the Institution of Mechanical Engineers, 27 April 1983.

42 Beenstock, *op. cit.*, pp.210 – 17.

43 Freeman *et al.*, *op. cit.*, p.134.

44 J. Elliott, 'The Cult of the Gifted Amateur', *Financial Times*, 5 May 1983.

45 P. Maunder (ed.), *Government Intervention in the Developed Economy* (1979), p.143.

46 There is a vast literature, but most of it points to the same conclusion; see in particular, D. K. Stout, in C. Carter (ed.), *Industrial Policy and Innovation* (1981), p.123; P. Mottershead, 'Industrial Policy', in F. Blackaby (ed.), *British Economic Policy 1960 – 1974* (1978), pp.482 – 3; *The Economist*, 4 March 1978, p.10; L. G. Manison, 'Some Factors Influencing the United Kingdom's Economic Growth Performance', *IMF Staff Papers*, **25** (1979), p.738; M. C. Fleming 'Industrial Policy', in P. Maunder (ed.), *The British Economy in the 1970s* (1980), pp.163 – 4. Fleming notes that intervention may even retard improvements in the efficiency of existing firms if companies begin to direct their attention and policies towards securing the maximum assistance from the government.

47 See C. C. Allen, 'Industrial Policy and Innovation in Japan', in C. Carter (ed.), *Industrial Policy and Innovation* (1981), pp.85-6.

48 K. Hawkins, *Unemployment* (1979), p.96.
49 G. Maynard, 'Microeconomic Deficiencies in UK Macroeconomic Policy', *Lloyds Bank Review*, **145** (1982), p.14.
50 C. M. Cooper and J. A. Clark, *Employment, Economics and Technology* (1982), pp.31, 110 – 11, 118.
51 K. Williams, J. Williams and D. Thomas, *Why Are the British Bad at Manufacturing?* (1982), pp.14 – 15.
52 In the late 1950s manufactured exports were 2½ – 3 times greater than manufactured imports (in value); by the early 1980s the difference was marginal (5 – 10 per cent), and currently manufactured imports are overtaking exports for the first time in recorded history. Manufactures now account for some two-thirds of total imports as against 20-25 per cent in the 1950s. Without oil exports Britain could not pay for her food and raw materials since the surplus on services (invisibles) is quite small. Any strong increase in domestic activity would therefore put severe pressure on the external account since not only would raw material imports increase, but so too would imports of manufactures given the high income elasticity of demand for imported manufactures. These could only be accommodated by raising the volume of manufactured exports.
53 Williams *et al.*, *op. cit.*, p.6.

5 Problems of Regional Imbalance

Regional differences in unemployment have been a marked feature of both the nineteenth and twentieth centuries. Before 1914 it was London and the southern counties of England which had relatively high levels of unemployment, whereas most of the northern regions (as well as Wales and Scotland) experienced more or less full employment on the back of the continued strength of their staple trades. After the first world war, when the latter collapsed, the position was reversed and for the remainder of the twentieth century it has been the North which has persistently recorded higher rates of unemployment than the national average. The North–South disparity was probably at its worst in the 1930s, but it remained prominent in the era of full employment, and it is only in more recent years, when unemployment generally approached the levels of the 1930s, that some narrowing of the differential occurred.[1] As might be expected, the persistence of this regional imbalance prompted governments to intervene increasingly in regional affairs from the 1930s onwards.

The main purpose of this chapter is to explain why regional imbalance tends to persist over time, or why, in other words, capital and labour do not flow in reverse directions so as to restore equilibrium among regions, albeit possibly at below full employment. The final section assesses the merits of the policy options for dealing with regional imbalance.

CONVERGENCE VERSUS REGIONAL IMBALANCE

Given an initial imbalance between regions in incomes and

employment, one might expect that, in a relatively free market, forces of convergence would eventually lead to a restoration of equilibrium. This might arise as follows. First, according to the neo-classical model, factors of production would flow in such a way as to bring about equilibrium: thus labour would move from low- to high-wage regions, while capital would flow in the reverse direction, providing that wages and the marginal product of capital were inversely correlated. One would then expect low-wage regions to grow fastest. Secondly, mature, high-income regions may suffer from agglomeration diseconomies and scarce resources, especially labour and physical space, while the scope for inter-sectoral resource shifts may be limited. This would tend to slow down growth in these regions and encourage firms to look for greenfield sites in areas where resources were more plentiful and cheaper. Thirdly, low-income regions have more to gain from sectoral resource reallocation, involving a movement of resources from low-wage, low-productivity sectors to high-wage, high-productivity ones, thereby raising income per head and improving the growth prospects of such regions.

While some transfer of factors along the lines specified in the neo-classical model have certainly occurred in the past,[2] forces of convergence have clearly not been strong otherwise there would be no regional problem. Distortions to the free market mechanism may partly account for the weakness of convergence factors, but it does fully explain why forces of divergence have predominated for much of the period and which have favoured the southern half of Britain, especially the south-east. The process of regional development may therefore be more accurately captured by the spatial shifts in economic activity reflected in the centre – periphery model, which stresses the way in which cumulative forces tend to favour centrally located, prosperous regions. Such a model would appear to be of significant relevance in explaining, for example, the increasing importance of the south-east and the Midlands as centres for manufacturing in the twentieth century, and the concomitant decline in regions further north. The shift in industrial activity from North to South was particularly marked in the inter-war period which saw the rise of the newer industries; between 1924 and 1935 the southern and Midland regions increased their share of net industrial output from 44.6 to 57.3 per cent, while all other regions, including Scotland and Wales, declined in relative importance (see Table 5.1). This increasing disparity was reflected in unemployment (see Chapter 1) and income levels, though for this period there are no regional income figures except for Scotland. These show that real income per head in Scotland rose by only 16 per cent between 1924 and 1938 compared with a national increase of about one-third, while the absolute level of income per head in Scotland was about 10 per cent lower than the average for Britain as a whole, and up to 20 per cent less in the early 1930s.[3] In the post-war period regional income differentials, though narrowing slightly, have persisted so that by the end of the 1970s the south-east had a level of disposable income per capita 11 per cent higher than the UK average and between 15 – 20 per cent above the levels of the lowest income regions, Scotland, Wales and the North of England.[4]

TABLE 5.1: **Percentage of Total Net Industrial Output in Census of Production Regions, 1924-35**

	1924	*1935*
Greater London	17.1	24.8
South-east, south-west and Midland counties (incl. part of North)	15.9	20.2
Warwick, Worcs. and Staffs.	11.6	12.3
Lancashire and Cheshire	20.8	15.5
West Riding of Yorks.	12.6	10.1
Northumberland and Durham	5.9	4.3
Wales	5.9	3.9
Scotland	10.2	8.9

Source: Political and Economic Planning, *Report on the Location of Industry in Great Britain* (1939), p.44.

REGIONAL DETERMINANTS OF ENTERPRISE
LOCATION

The forces which have prompted capital and economic activity
to gravitate to the South and at the same time deterred capital
and enterprise from moving into the poorer regions[5] may be
conveniently discussed under the following headings: (1)
market accessibility; (2) labour supply advantages; (3) agglomeration economies; (4) quality of infrastructure facilities, for
example transport; and (5) structural characteristics. The rest
of this section will be devoted to exploring the locational
determinants of enterprise against the background of the
North – South differential; while the subsequent section will
deal with the impediments to labour mobility.

One of the more important determinants of location is that
of market accessibility. Though the advantages of particular
market locations have never been clearly specified, there seem
to be good grounds for arguing that the location of manufacturing activity in close proximity to major markets has
become of increasing importance in the twentieth century. As
the old staple export trades declined, so too did the importance
of energy and raw material sources and access to ports and rail
links as determinants of location. The rise of the consumer
goods industries, the growth of road transport and the spread
of new forms of power, for example oil and electricity, meant
that industry became more foot-loose and ubiquitous, and its
pattern of trade flows more dispersed and oriented towards the
consumer market. Consequently, a central location within
easy reach of the main markets became of increasing importance to enterprise. In terms of the quality and size of
market the south-east and Midlands clearly have spatial
attractions with which no other region can bear comparison.
Roughly one-half of the population of the UK is located in the
south-east (including East Anglia) and the Midlands, while the
central position of the Midland counties is convenient for
market catchment further north – the northern, north-west
and Yorkshire and Humberside regions which account for a
further 25 per cent of Britain's population. The quality of the
southern market is also attractive, especially that of the south-

east where personal incomes and consumer spending are considerably higher than in northern Britain (see above). Moreover, a southern or central location not only provides easy access to the main regional markets, but also to European and international markets given the good communications and financial and institutional facilities in the southern half of the country.

Transport costs are also relevant in this context. While it is true that for a large part of manufacturing such costs comprise only around 3 per cent of the value of gross output, there are some significant variations between industries and areas.[6] Bulky, fragile and perishable goods tend to be costly to transport; a notable example is furniture, which partly explains why the industry is heavily concentrated in the south-east of England. Thus, for locations in the far North serving distant markets, the incidence of transport dues for such products can be considerable which may limit the viability of operations given the small regional market available. In general the least cost locations with respect to transport costs in serving the national market are in the south-east and Midlands, while the highest occur in the North, Scotland and East Anglia. A further point to bear in mind is that most manufacturers include transport costs in the price of the finished products, and quote a uniform delivered price to all customers, a practice which tends to favour locations close to the main markets. Distant locations may also impose other costs, for example, the need to hold larger stocks requiring greater working capital, and the danger of delays and disruptions at terminal points in transit.

While many locational decisions in manufacturing would appear to arise from random or personal factors, for example, the owner setting up business close to his place of residence and without serious consideration of the cost of alternative sites, nevertheless many manufacturers, both before and after the war, cite the importance of ready access to good markets, and not only for reasons of size and quality. A convenient central location may be essential from the point of view of securing prompt and easy contact with customers, suppliers, subcontractors and professional and financial services in order to acquire the maximum information about markets, prices, the competitive climate, and the like. One would not necessarily expect of course that market convenience would attract large flows of itinerant entrepreneurs from the border regions to the central location; rather its primary function may be simply to provide a congenial environment in which native talent and enterprise thrive to the best advantage. On the other hand, from a market point of view, there seems little in the northern regions to attract the budding entrepreneur to establish operations there.

If the northern regions are disadvantageously placed marketwise, it might be thought that they would stand to gain from the labour supply side. Given the presence of higher unemployment, the labour supply should be more elastic and wages lower than in the South. But there is much more to the labour problem than the mere counting of heads, while the labour cost advantage is far from clear cut. The south-east and Midlands are frequently cited favourably as areas where the quality and skills of the labour force are good and varied, and where the efficiency, reliability and productivity of the workforce is better than elsewhere. Industrial relations are also better than in the North where the strong and entrenched position of the unions is reflected in the more conservative attitude to work and innovation, and in the higher rate of absenteeism. Moreover, if the South scores in terms of the quality of its labour force, it is not at all clear that the North can offer appreciably lower labour costs as an inducement. In fact, nationally negotiated rates of pay and standard tax and benefit rates have limited the scope for marked regional variations in earnings and labour costs. Data for average hourly earnings of full-time manual workers and for total labour costs are given in Table 5.2. These show that while the south-east tends to be a high cost area, average hourly earnings were higher in both the North of England and Wales, and that only the south-west and East Anglia had noticeably lower hourly earnings than the national average. As for total labour costs, the south-east is again high, but with Wales close behind, while the lowest total costs are recorded in the East Midlands, East Anglia, Yorkshire and Humberside and Scotland. A note of caution should be added when interpreting these statistics; those for total labour costs include the effect of regional

99

subsidies which should widen any differential between North and South; secondly, they refer to an average of different trades and therefore the figures for each region will reflect its specific occupational distribution. However, similar data for individual industries do not appear to alter the main conclusions to any significant extent. On balance, taking into account both cost and quality differentials, the North would seem to have little to offer on the labour side to induce new business and capital to locate in the poorer regions.

Capital will also tend to move in the wrong direction for convergence as a result of the self-sustaining agglomeration economies accruing to high income regions. The benefits of

TABLE 5.2: **Earnings and Labour Costs in Manufacturing**

	Average Hourly Earnings of Full-time Manual Men (pence per hour) (April 1979)	*Total Labour Costs in Manufacturing (pence per hour) (1975)*[1]
Great Britain	197.5	161.68
North	203.7	164.81
Yorkshire and Humberside	197.7	153.43
East Midlands	196.7	147.80
East Anglia	189.2	153.11
South-east	200.3	173.37
South-west	181.7	158.18
West Midlands	201.8	160.62
North-west	196.7	158.97
England	197.6	161.88
Wales	202.4	172.54
Scotland	194.1	153.38

Note: 1 Includes wage and salary costs, taxes, insurance contributions and welfare benefits, and the effects of subsidies.

Source: Regional Statistics (1979, 1981).

agglomeration can be quite considerable since the linkages between firms and industries in a mature economy are very close, with a large part of manufacturing output being sold to industrial customers. External economies for the individual firm may also be of significance in areas where it is possible to draw readily upon ancillary services, for example banking, financial and professional services of the metropolitan region, and where there exists a wide range of specialist suppliers and sub-contractors. Thus, for example, the growth of the car industry in the Midlands has been accompanied by a parallel expansion in component firms supplying the inputs for car assembly, whereas the establishment of motor manufacturing in Scotland had relatively little impact in this respect because the scale of operations was too small, with the result that many of the components were imported from other regions.[7] The rate of technical progress and innovation also tends to be higher in more prosperous regions as a result of higher savings, investment and R & D expenditure and an industrial structure weighted in favour of products with a high income elasticity of demand. Furthermore, innovational change and diffusion may be more pronounced in these regions because of the ease of entry for new firms (see below) and to the fact that 'The recipients of new techniques, that is high-calibre managers, tend to be disproportionately concentrated in wealthy metropolitan regions and are often unwilling to move to less developed regions suffering from inferior social and cultural environments.'[8] Against these advantages must be offset the diseconomies of agglomeration through congestion, over-crowding, high rental and residential costs and the time and costs involved in travelling between home and work place. Such diseconomies are more relevant to the south-east than the Midland regions.

As regards infrastructure facilities, transport, public services, educational provision and residential accommodation, the South again scores over the North. This is especially the case with respect to communications. In terms of the quality and range of road, rail and air services and access to port facilities the southern and Midland regions, especially the latter, are better placed than those further north. Most of the major transport improvements, especially road and rail, during the last decade or so have been designed to serve the needs of this part of the country, in the broad belt between London and Manchester. These improvements have further enhanced the degree of accessibility of these regions in terms of national and international markets. The same could be said of the inter-war years and even farther back in time; in the coaching era of the eighteenth century it was London and the south-east whence radiated the main network of coach services.

Finally, we turn to the composition of industrial structure and its influence on regional performance. For much of the twentieth century the northern regions of Britain have suffered from an unfavourable industrial structure which has slowed down their growth and imposed barriers to the entry of new firms. After the first world war the large staple trades of the nineteenth century – mining, textiles, shipbuilding, mechanical engineering – underwent permanent contraction resulting from a combination of unfavourable factors including changing demand patterns, declining competitiveness, tariffs and other trade barriers. Given the strong geographic concentration of the staple industries in the North of England, Scotland and Wales, it is not surprising that these regions fared so much worse than the South which benefited from the growth of the new consumer trades, services and a buoyant housing market arising from population shifts.

Scotland may be taken as a good example of the vulnerability from exposure to an unbalanced industrial structure. The staple industries accounted for 43.2 and 36.8 per cent of net industrial output in 1924 and 1935 respectively, as against 37 and 27.8 per cent for the country as a whole, while Scotland's share in the new growth industries (vehicles, electrical engineering, rayon, non-ferrous metals and paper, publishing and printing) accounted for 8.3 and 11 per cent of her industrial output in these years compared with national averages of 14.1 and 21 per cent. Scotland's problem resulted from the dramatic collapse of export demand for her staple products; the volume of exports through Scottish ports fell by 56 per cent between 1913 and 1933, and even at the peak of recovery they were still 42 per cent below the pre-war level. Heavy concentration on declining basic sectors resulted in depressed growth and lower productivity and real income per head than the rest of the country, which in turn affected the performance of local and service industries and discouraged the development of new and expanding sectors of the economy.[9]

A similar pattern was repeated in other northern regions, where in some areas the old staples accounted for up to 60 – 70 per cent of the insured labour force.[10] In the South, with its more favourable locational advantages and its more diversified industrial structure, the pressure was eased by the rapid development in new consumer trades and services, though even here of course the growth of employment was insufficient to cope with both local unemployment and the drift of workers from the North.

Despite some improvement in the industrial composition of the northern regions they have continued to suffer a disadvantage in this respect compared with the South throughout the post-war period. Not surprisingly, therefore, they have again borne the brunt of recent redundancies. An analysis by Martin for 1980 shows that whereas below average rates of labour shake-out occurred in the south-east, East Anglia, the south-west and the East Midlands, all other regions had above average redundancy rates. In contrast to the former group, all northern regions and Wales experienced losses on account of both industrial composition and region specific effects.[11] It is also significant that in the depressed areas of Britain – which now includes the West Midlands – manufacturing tends to be characterised by large-sized or branch plants, higher labour costs relative to net output, and a greater proportion of old or ageing capital stock than in the South and East, and this imbalance helps to explain the differential rate of employment decline within many industries as between North and South. Because of these characteristics the peripheral regions have borne the brunt of the streamlining and de-manning carried out by many of the large multi-plant enterprises. This means that the job prospects of the depressed regions in any revival of the economy may be limited by dint of the fact that much of the rationalisation reflects cost and efficiency improvements of a permanent nature. This could have important implications for regional policy.

Not only has the unfavourable industrial structure of the

northern regions inhibited their growth potential, but it has also presented these regions with a problem in terms of attracting new enterprises. The dynamics of regional growth suggest that structural format can exercise considerable influence on locational decisions. A diversified and flexible industrial structure which permits the frequent entry and exit of firms is likely to be more conducive to regional prosperity than an inflexible structure dominated by one or two firms or industries. Sustained growth and transformation are dependent on the rate at which new firms can develop both in old and new sectors, a fact borne out by the remarkable structural transformation and resilience of the East Midland region since the war, where a diversified though initially unfavourable industrial structure favoured a high entry rate of new firms.[12] At the same time the ease with which entry can be made is partly conditioned by the industrial structure. Where this is fairly diversified with a large number of small and medium-sized plants and firms covering a wide range of industries, it permits a far greater degree of flexibility than in regions heavily comitted to one or two product groups and/or dominated by large firms. Thus the northern regions, with their heavy commitment to one or two ex-growth staples and the presence of large conservative firms, have lacked the flexibility of the South's diversified structure, and this in turn has deterred the development of new enterprises, both indigenous and in-migrating.[13] In fact regional disparities in growth and development may be seen as

a microcosm of inter-country disparities with their related vicious and virtuous circle effects. Regions or countries with rigid and inflexible structures resulting partly from overdependence on a limited number of activities experience difficulty in attracting new developments, which would help to diversify their structures, because the barriers to entry are high, whereas regions or countries with well-balanced structural profiles and many small firms in growing trades, are conducive to enterprise, which in turn helps to maintain the vitality of their economies.[14]

The foregoing discussion points to the conclusion that since the first world war the southern half of the country has provided a more receptive environment for enterprise and risk-taking than the North, where the economic and institutional structure has for too long retained a hangover from its nineteenth-century experience, which has tended to stifle new enterprise.[15] In terms of market potential, infrastructure facilities, the quality of the labour force, agglomeration benefits and industrial structure, the South, especially the south-east, has consistently scored over the northern regions.[16] On the other hand, the South's attractions when converted into monetary costs, may not be all that substantial; it has been estimated that for three-quarters of manufacturing activity the spatial margins to profitable production do not exist to any considerable extent in the UK, which suggests that they can scarcely be a crucial determinant of location.[17] However, since both first-time and established entrepreneurs are frequently unaware of the comparative costs of alternative locations, it may well be that subjective perception of the comparative merits between North and South has a stronger influence than purely cost considerations would warrant. And after all, this is what counts in the final analysis. As Sir Malcolm Stewart, Special Areas Commissioner for England and Wales, found in a survey of 5800 firms conducted in 1935, very few – precisely eight out of the total – were even prepared to consider investing in the special areas designated under the legislation of 1934. The reasons cited for not so doing are familiar – inaccessibility, low consumer purchasing power, high unionisation and heavy local taxes.[18]

LABOUR MOBILITY

If capital does not move in the way the convergence theory postulates, then the alternatives to capital transfer must be considered: the movement of workers from the poorer to the richer regions, and the adjustment of regional wage differentials in favour of the depressed areas. Though a high degree of labour mobility is often regarded as essential to an expanding economy, broadly speaking the main thrust of regional policy has been one of bringing work to the workers. While a policy of attempting to achieve regional balance may be justified from a social point of view, the doctrine of regional balance has been challenged on the grounds of efficiency and effectiveness. Pitfield, for example, in a study of inter-war labour migration cautioned against using a policy of diverting industry into areas of high unemployment if it entailed detrimental consequences for its efficiency.[19] For the post-war period, Richardson and West raise doubts as to the merits of the regional balance doctrine as the most effective way of reducing unemployment. Historical experience suggests that differential growth rates between sectors and regions are to be expected and that to aim at steady inter-regional development may involve sacrificing growth for stability. Moreover, the authors also question the moral right of condemning the unemployed in the development districts to the ranks of an industrial reserve army 'in the vain hope that its size will whet the appetites of sufficient industrialists to ensure that unemployment levels are brought down to the national average.[20]

It might be questioned whether labour transfer is a practical proposition in times of mass unemployment when job availability rather than regional income differentials is likely to be the crucial factor in determining a worker's decision to migrate. When jobs are scarce nationally there would seem to be little point in incurring the upheaval and cost of removal. However, this is to miss the point of the whole issue. Though at the depth of the depression jobs are hard to come by anywhere, as soon as recovery gets under way shortages of labour begin to develop in certain occupations, trades and regions, which often cannot be filled readily from the unemployment reserves. Thus by the mid-1930s, severe shortages of labour, especially of skilled workers in the South, were being reported by many trades, including building, engineering, electrical manufacturing and aircraft production.[21] Similarly, every upturn in activity since the second world war has been accompanied by complaints of shortages of skilled labour, particularly in the engineering industry, while even at the present time shortages are apparent in some sectors, notably in electronics.[22]

That such shortages should develop amidst plenty is to be explained by the complex heterogeneity of the labour market and the uneven pattern of growth. The process of growth and development is not based on a static structure, it is one of continual change. Thus the composition of employment is in a state of perpetual flux as trades and occupations thrive and perish, and as the frontiers of technology change. Inevitably, this gives rise from time to time to a skill mismatch between labour supply and demand. Similarly, as the regional incidence of growth and structural change varies, so too will the occupational structure; some regions will experience labour shortages in particular occupations and skills, while others will accumulate large labour reserves. Under these conditions no amount of unemployment and labour mobility can solve the basic mismatch problem, namely the need to retrain and re-equip redundant workers with new skills. As the authors of a study of the engineering labour market in London in the latter half of 1936 commented:

There is no force in the argument that, because engineers are to be found registered as unemployed, there must be a slack to be taken up in this market. The demand for engineering labour is not a simple and straightforward quantity; it is of varied and ever-changing pattern. Unless the quality of supply can be readily adapted, there will be unemployment irrespective of the amount of supply.[23]

In other words, the wrong skill mix of Britain's jobless may partly explain the low level of labour mobility in the 1930s and 1980s. Many redundant workers had little prospect of taking up employment in different occupations and regions unless they could acquire new skills, the opportunities for which were very limited in the 1930s, and even in the post-war period it was not until the 1970s that retraining programmes were developed on an extensive scale. Even then the opportunities for older workers to re-equip with new skills are somewhat limited.

The problem of retraining apart, labour mobility in Britain has been traditionally weak for other reasons. Most workers regard the labour market as essentially a local one. The Department of Employment's 1974 survey found that the majority of unemployed men in most regions were unwilling to move anywhere beyond a daily travelling distance.[24] The marked social inertia of the British working class is particularly prevalent in the depressed northern regions where the cohesion and resilience of tight-knit communities have created social exit barriers of considerable strength. It has resulted in

a marked unwillingness to break out of the tight-knit cultural and social environment built up by the industrial working class in the nineteenth century and which now controlled and sustained them. Chapel, club and trade union did survive. Organisations to help the unemployed grew from local roots. If anything, especially in small towns, the more severe the depression the closer the community grew; unemployment was a shared experience and the financial and moral support of family, friends and local institutions persuaded many to stay. These were the ties which dissuaded most people from risking greater distress by leaving.[25]

While this description refers specifically to the 1930s, the social ties which bind workers to their local communities are still strong today, though no doubt weakened by the passage of time.

Financial considerations are also an important factor to take into account when contemplating migration. The cost of changing job and residence may be unprofitable, especially since it will usually involve a shift to an area of more expensive housing in the South. Moreover, according to a recent study, Britain's housing policies have drastically reduced the migration rate of a large segment of the population.[26] Rent control and security of tenure in the private housing market have led to a long-term decline in the supply of rented accommodation. But the principal impediment stems from the fact that a large proportion of the housing stock consists of subsidised council houses; Britain has one of the highest shares of public housing in the world, at around one-third of the total, and considerably higher in some of the poorer areas. This, together with the uniform system of social security and rent and rate rebates, effectively locks people into particular areas. Unless intending migrants can find similar accommodation at the same cost in the areas of destination – not an easy task under present local authority housing administration[27] – there may be little financial incentive to encourage movement. A similar situation occurred in the inter-war years as a result of the rising stock of council houses and the system of rent control of working-class dwellings: 'In the absence of perfect information about the availability and price of accommodation in other parts of the country, the incentive to stay put was strong.'[28]

Finally, regional wage differentials merit attention in this context. What is noticeable, both in the inter-war period and in the last decade, is the relative absence of marked variations in wages between regions. Broadly speaking, wages in areas of high unemployment have not been very responsive to the large excess supplies of labour. Thus throughout the inter-war years industrial and regional wage differentials showed little tendency to increase,[29] while more recently, as noted earlier, current regional wage differentials are quite small and certainly do not fully reflect regional variations in the state of the labour market.[30] The reasons for this lack of flexibility are twofold. One is that the unions have been anxious to maintain a nationally negotiated system of wage rates even at the expense of employment, and the strength of organised labour in the depressed regions has enabled the unions to avoid trading wages against unemployment.[31] Secondly, because tax and benefit rates are identical between regions it has effectively put a national floor under non-union wages. The consequences are that regional variations in demand and union power are not reflected in a decline in non-union wages in depressed regions with the result that these regions respond with differentially increased unemployment.[32] The failure to depress wages and incomes (via benefits) in areas of high unemployment tends both to reduce the degree of labour mobility and limit the ability of employers to recruit more workers.

REGIONAL POLICY

It is generally recognised that macro-economic policy cannot by itself provide an adequate solution to regional imbalance. Keynes himself, in the first of his now famous series of articles to *The Times* early in 1937, felt the time was approaching when

there is not much advantage in applying a further general stimulus to the centre. So long as surplus resources were widely diffused between industries and localities it was no great matter at what point in the economic structure the impulse of an increased demand was applied. But the evidence grows that ... the economic structure is unfortunately rigid, that (for example) building activity in the home counties is less effective than one might have hoped in decreasing unemployment in the distressed areas. It follows that the later stages of

109

recovery require a different technique. To remedy the condition of the distressed areas, *ad hoc* measures are necessary ... We are more in need to-day of a rightly distributed demand than of a greater aggregate demand; and the Treasury would be entitled to economise elsewhere to compensate for the cost of special assistance to the distressed areas.[33]

Though nowadays one may quail at the reference to *ad hoc* measures, Keynes was aware, if belatedly, of the limitations of macro-policy and the need to discriminate in favour of the poorer regions. As Hawkins observes, 'It would be naive to assume that these structural problems can be solved simply by raising aggregate demand to an "appropriate level", or by introducing import controls, or by some other form of macro-economic wizardry.'[34] In fact macro-policy is too broad and blunt an instrument to tackle the structural problems of regional imbalance effectively and indeed it may tend to prolong them in so far as a general demand stimulus provides the present structural format of these regions with a new, but temporary, lease of life. Moreover, the weakness of the regional income multipliers, due to the size of the leakages to the rest of the economy and abroad, means that the depressed areas tend to experience a limited and belated benefit from any general upturn in activity, whereas the more dynamic regions soon become overheated.[35] On the other hand, the limitations in this context should not obscure the fact that a satisfactory solution to the problems of regional disparity may depend upon a prosperous national economy.[36] After all, some two-thirds of the jobs created through regional policy in the assisted areas in the last twenty years have been deported from the South and East of Britain to the poorer regions,[37] but at a time of high unemployment nationally these areas can no longer hope to provide surplus jobs.[38] Moreover, as Morley has shown, when the national share of gross profits in income increases, unemployment tends to decline most rapidly in regions where it is worst, from whence it follows that regional policies which detract from the level of national prosperity will be counter-productive.[39]

The question we must ask therefore is not simply whether regional policy has been successful in alleviating imbalance by creating more activity and jobs in the poorer regions, but whether it has accomplished this task without sacrificing the integrity of the national economy. To put it another way, could the resources which have been poured into the assisted areas have been put to alternative and better use, and thereby have produced a superior rate of return for the economy as a whole? Before attempting to answer this imposing question we must first outline briefly the principle elements of Britain's post-war regional policy.

The foundations of modern regional policy can be traced back to the inter-war years, starting in the later 1920s with the scheme of assisted labour transfer through to the special areas legislation of the 1930s which sought to generate jobs in a small number of depressed areas as opposed to trying to persuade workers to move to where employment was available. Neither policy managed to make much impression on the enormous spatial imbalance of labour reserves in the inter-war years, though the policy of stimulating labour mobility was more successful than the depressed areas legislation, which was very limited in scope and which only became effective rather late on in the period. Altogether, during the period 1928 – 38 some 280,000 individuals were transferred from the depressed areas to other regions through the employment exchanges, whereas in the latter half of the 1930s probably less than 50,000 new jobs were created as a result of the implementation of the special areas legislation (1934, 1937). However, it was the latter policy which provided the basis for the vast expansion in regional intervention in the post-war period.[40]

Though the intensity of regional policy has varied considerably since 1945, for much of the period the overall trend has been towards increasing the scale and the scope of regional intervention, at least until the recent cutbacks at the end of the 1970s. After a burst of activity under the Labour government in the later 1940s, though with a temporary cutback in 1947 following the financial crisis of that year, regional policy was allowed to lapse somewhat in the 1950s. During the 1960s and the first half of the 1970s (apart from a temporary reigning back in the early 1970s), regional policy was vastly extended until the financial crisis of 1976, after which the emphasis was switched to national issues and the problems of inner city areas. Subsequently, under the Thatcher Government of 1979, a massive cut in regional assistance was proposed. In real terms the growth of total government spending on regional policy has been impressive, rising from £34 million in the financial year 1960/1 (at 1975 prices) to a peak of £612 million in 1969/70, after which there was temporary fall in 1972/3 before peaking again at £611 million in 1975/6. It then tailed off somewhat before collapsing to £322 million in 1979/80 under the new policy direction.[41]

The avowed aim of regional policy has been to halt, or reverse, the growing disparity between regions in terms of unemployment, income and economic growth, and, as far as implementation is concerned, the emphasis has been throughout on taking work to the workers rather than on trying to induce workers to migrate to employment. Policy has therefore been heavily orientated towards providing inducements for firms to move or to expand in the depressed regions. The designated assisted areas have been continually redefined and extended by numerous pieces of legislation. The first areas selected were the pre-war special areas (South Wales, Northeast England, West Cumberland and Central Scotland) and in the later 1940s these were extended to cover fairly large development areas. They were replaced in 1960 by development districts based on local employment exchange areas, and their number was greatly increased early in 1966 as a prelude to a return to the concept of the large development area later in that year. The new development areas accounted for some 20 per cent of the country's population, about twice that of the former development districts. This percentage was raised slightly in the following year with the designation of special development areas, which were zones lying within the large development areas. Far more important however was the introduction of intermediate area status at the turn of the decade which encompassed a population of similar size to that of the existing assisted areas. These were areas lying outside the main development areas but suffering similar problems, but as yet in a less acute form.

Thus by the 1970s assisted area designation of one sort or another covered a substantial part of the country, accounting for some 43 – 4 per cent of Great Britain's population. Apart from Northern Ireland, which has always been treated as a special case, the development areas included all of Scotland and the North, Yorkshire and Humberside, North Devon and Cornwall, and Wales except for certain eastern fringes. Special development area status was accorded to west-central Scotland, Tyneside and Wear, West Cumberland, Merseyside and parts of North and South Wales; while intermediate area status included the Chesterfield area, parts of Devon and the remaining areas of Wales and north-west England. The Conservative Government's plans for collapsing the scale of the regional programme involved a reduction in the area designated for assistance from 43 – 4 per cent of the population to 25 per cent by 1983, by downgrading or abolishing many former assisted areas, and a reduction in the level of support grants to the areas remaining. It was projected that total regional spending would be reduced by about two-fifths, and that the remaining expenditure would be made more cost-effective by concentrating it on areas of greatest need.[42]

To effect a transfer of resources to the assisted regions a series of different policy instruments has been enforced; the details of these and the intensity of their application have been changed frequently and only the main outlines can be given here. First, there is the direct and negative control of the Industrial Development Certificate (IDC). This was introduced in 1947 and any industrial development above a certain minimum size had to obtain one before planning permission could be considered. They were only readily issued for projects in the assisted areas while after 1966 their issue was tightly controlled in the Midlands and south-east. From 1972 they were no longer required in the development areas and two years later a three-tier system of approval was introduced for the non-assisted areas, though by that time the rigidity of the control system was beginning to wane under the impact of the recession.

The second major instrument has been the blanket subsidies or financial incentives designed to induce firms to develop in the assisted areas. They comprise a whole series of complex differential grants and allowances to encourage investment in plant, buildings and machinery, the provisions of which have been changed frequently. In addition, the Regional Employment Premium (REP) was introduced in 1967. This was a direct and unconditional subsidy paid to all firms in the development areas per employee per week with different rates for men, women and juveniles. Originally it was intended that it should be phased out by the mid-1970s, but the premium was still being paid by the end of that decade. It has proved to be a somewhat expensive way of maintaining employment in the assisted regions, and in 1975–6 it accounted for about one-third of all public expenditure on regional assistance.

Thirdly, in addition to the general subsidies, there has been a series of selective subsidies, notably those under the Industry Act 1972 to prevent plant closure, together with various forms of *ad hoc* assistance given to nationalised industries and private firms in an effort to prop up ailing sectors or firms in the depressed regions.

Fourthly, the government has been active in providing new factory space in the poorer regions. Since the war public agencies have built over 1000 new factories in the assisted areas. This has been one of the more successful parts of regional policy, especialy in terms of attracting small firms, while the cost involved is often quite modest given the fact that many of the factories produce a rental income or are eventually sold to the occupants.

Finally, in more general terms, the development regions have benefited from government provision of infrastructure such as roads, bridges, drainage and community facilities, measures of land reclamation, clearance of derelict sites and the sponsorship of new industrial estates, including the latest enterprise zones.[43]

The poorer regions can scarcely complain therefore that they have been neglected in the post-war period. The scope and scale of regional provision has been extensive and it would be surprising had they failed to derive some visible benefit from it. In fact there is fairly general agreement that the major instruments of regional policy have been successful in terms of stimulating or diverting employment, investment and the movement of firms into the designated areas. However, it is difficult to provide precise estimates as to their impact because of the lack of consensus among investigators and the fragmented time periods over which various studies have been conducted.[44] As far as investment is concerned one may state that, in broad terms, regional policy has had a noticeable effect in diverting investment to the regions in question. Between 1968 and 1974, for example, approximately 60 per cent of all manufacturing investment in the UK was made by establishments in the assisted areas, and regional policy was responsible for a sizeable shift in the share of investment towards these areas. Rees and Miall estimate that in the years 1975 – 8 the average measured shift to three development areas (Wales, the North and Scotland) was of the order of 6.9 per cent, which may be regarded as quite substantial when set against the base period share of 23 per cent for these regions.[45] On the employment front it would seem that upwards of 350,000 jobs have been shifted in favour of the assisted areas in the decade and a half to 1980, though this was only sufficient to reduce the imbalance between jobs and the growth of population in these areas by about one-quarter.[46]

In terms of the investment diversion to the assisted areas, the job generation impact does not appear all that impressive. Despite the expenditure of very large sums, regional policy has done little more than stabilise the situation; it has not been effective in reversing the disparity between the regions and none of the depressed areas has achieved rates of growth of output or structural change faster than the UK average. As Morris noted in 1979 'there is little sign that assistance, even if it is maintained at the present level, will bring about overall regional balance or make a very significant contribution to the growth of industrial productivity.'[47] Perhaps more disturbing is the suspicion that the administration of regional policy is not all it could have been. The Trade and Industry Sub-Committee of the House of Commons Expenditure Committee, reporting at the end of 1973, was highly critical of the government's regional policy. It was felt that 'Much has been spent and much may well have been wasted. Regional policy has been empiricism run mad, a game of hit-and-miss, played with more enthusiasm than success.' The Committee deplored the frequent changes in policy and the failure to assess the impact of different policy options,[48] and it urged the government to create 'a more rational and systematic basis for the formulation and execution of regional policy.'[49] In the light of Britain's national priorities it may well be that regional policy was misconceived and that an alternative strategy would have produced better results.

There are several detailed criticisms that can be made about individual policy instruments, but for the most part we shall confine the discussion to the ways in which regional policy has detracted from more important national objectives, namely growth, efficiency and structural change, such that the underlying competitive strength of the economy is impaired.

Assuming that the principle national objective is to improve the competitive efficiency of the economy, then if productivity levels are found to be lower in the assisted areas any attempt to divert resources to these areas will reduce the overall growth potential of the economy. In a detailed inter-regional productivity study for the 1970s, Cameron found that the south-east had a clear productivity lead over other regions in nearly all the major sectors of manufacturing activity, as well as in many branches of engineering and in the high potential growth sectors of the economy. The only other area which approached the south-east in terms of productivity strength in depth was East Anglia. It follows, therefore, that if the main objective is to improve the international competitiveness of manufacturing industry, assistance should be given to those firms and sectors which are already commercially strong rather than using scarce national resources in helping weak companies to move nearer the margin of competitiveness, since the marginal returns from a given injection of investment in sectors with a relatively high level of productivity are likely to be greater than from those with below average performance. The prescription for regional policy can then be written accordingly:

If certain industries have generated externalities in particular areas that permit high productivity performance, IDC policy should continually recognise this fact and only seek diversions to other regions if there is unequivocal evidence of unacceptable local social costs flowing from new developments in the South East and/or clear evidence that operating costs in the assisted areas are likely to be no higher, without subsidy, within a relatively short project-installation period. In this context we have provided some illustrations where the productivity advantage of the South East is so marked that it would make nonsense of an Industrial Strategy, which seeks competitiveness and rapid growth, to encourage companies to engage in the time-consuming process of establishing new assisted-area plants[50]

When one looks more closely at the application of regional policies it becomes clear that there are a wide range of adverse side-effects including subsidisation of inefficient firms, industrial diseconomies arising from split locations, and the discouragement of rationalisation and labour mobility, all of which can lead to a loss of national growth. As yet no comprehensive analysis has been made of the opportunity costs of regional assistance but it is possible to indicate some of the directions in which it has proved harmful. For example, the blanket capital and labour subsidies have been paid to efficient and inefficient firms alike and no attempt has been made to discriminate the allocation of assistance on the basis of potential export performance (or import saving) or the contribution to new technology. Morley also argues that many of the regional subsidies have had a rather limited impact on the assisted areas owing to the fact that their allocative signals have been lost in the noise created by inflation and too many changes in policy, the overall effect of which is to increase uncertainty and reduce profits, investment and employment.[51] The uncertainty created by frequent policy changes was particularly marked in the 1960s. Between 1960 and 1967 six major sets of changes in regional policy were announced and seven Acts substantially affecting industry's fortunes in the less prosperous regions were passed; the boundaries of areas entitled to receive special assistance were altered four times while administrative policies and practices were changed five times. Not surprisingly industrialists were confused about the benefits to which they were entitled and uncertain as to their permanence such that a CBI regional study concluded that 'the uncertainty of their duration and availability has led firms to discount them for the purposes of long-term planning.'[52] It is difficult to say exactly how far direct control through IDC applications has led to the uneconomic location of plants and choked off investment and expansion in the more prosperous areas. Since a considerable proportion of manufacturing industry is foot-loose with regard to location costs, it may be inferred that this has not been a major problem. However, the initial start-up costs in the assisted areas are far from negligible, while it is significant that regional policy tended to aggravate the 'size without scale' problem in so far as many large firms were encouraged or compelled to open branch factories in the North and West, and it was often these plants which were the first to be closed or rationalised when the economic climate deteriorated.[53] There is also evidence to indicate that when IDC control was applied more stringently, many schemes for development in the south-east and Midlands for which development certificates were required were either abandoned, deferred or modified as an alternative to accepting approved locations in the assisted areas.[54]

From the point of view of the long-term viability of the depressed regions themselves, regional policy has done little to overcome their initial disadvantages. It has not transformed them into high-growth, technological bases largely because policy in general has been focused on maintaining employment at the cost of structural transformation. This has meant that substantial resources have been directed towards helping unsuccessful and uneconomic firms in traditional sectors which has tended to ossify the industrial structure of the regions most in need of transformation. A recent conference on Industrial Policy and Innovation concluded that governments tend to spend far more on preventing industrial change by bolstering up dying and incompetent enterprises than they do on promoting innovation and structural change.[55] Only about 10 per cent of the total spending of about £2 billion a year in support of industry (end of the 1970s) was designed to assist directly the process of industrial change.[56] Politically, the temptation to help 'lame ducks' in the depressed areas has been too strong to resist, and so already vulnerable sectors such as coal, shipbuilding and iron and steel, received a new lease of life through the injection of substantial public funds into these regions. In some cases, such policies entailed the uneconomic location of plants in order to preserve employment.

Steel is a classic case with a long history, stretching back to the 1930s when Richard Thomas & Co were persuaded to locate their new strip mill at Ebbw Vale rather than in the Midlands, on to 1958 when, in the interests of regional employment, the then Prime Minister decided that new strip mill capacity should be divided equally between Scotland and

South Wales, leaving Britain with two sub-optimal mills, through to the agonising decisions on plant location and closure in the 1970s when the steel industry was still indifferently located.[57] But, as Wilson has pointed out, what was not considered by those who favoured aid to support the inefficient in the depressed regions was the effect this had on preserving the existing industrial structure, nor the wider implications for the economy as a whole in so far as 'similar measures might one day be extended well outside these areas, with a corresponding claim on limited public funds and with harmful implications over the long run for the national economy and the assisted areas themselves.' In this context the car industry provides a good example of the political impossibility of pouring money into Chrysler's loss-making plant in Scotland without doing the same for BL in the Midlands.[58]

Diversification of the economic structure of the assisted regions may also be retarded by the type of activity frequently enticed to these areas by regional policy. As already noted, it has attracted many branch plants to the assisted areas, which tend to carry on routine production functions with relatively low status jobs, whereas top management and decision-making on such matters as finance, marketing and R & D expenditure are performed outwith the regions, usually in London and the south-east. Scotland is perhaps the most notable example in this respect because of its high level of external ownership in manufacturing, the effect of which is to limit the range of skilled jobs and top management functions such as to induce personnel to seek better opportunities further south once a certain level of status has been reached. This in turn may inhibit the region's ability to generate new enterprises and job opportunities outside the manufacturing sector, for example, office employment, market research and finance, which would help to diversify the occupational structure.[59]

While it would be futile to deny that some regional support is necessary, it may be questioned whether the lavish expenditure of the past has been wholly beneficial either from a regional or national point of view. Regional assistance has often conflicted with national economic objectives in terms of growth and efficiency, while it has contributed very little to revitalise the regions in question. Indeed, the evidence presented would indicate that it has hindered the normal process of market adjustment, a point confirmed by Beenstock. 'Regional support', he argues,

may keep jobs going but unless the underlying situation alters it simply puts off the day of adjustment. As a region becomes uncompetitive, unemployment will tend to rise. The philosophy of past Conservative and Labour governments has been to provide regional aid in an attempt to bring regional unemployment rates down towards the averate. In this way some of the more depressed regions have become institutionalised by the very policies that were supposed to help them.[60]

In view of the high costs and indifferent success of post-war regional policy we feel there is a good case for a thorough overhaul of the administration of regional assistance measures. The accumulation of *ad hoc* and piecemeal schemes should be contained, and a more explicit analysis should be made of the costs and benefits of particular forms of assistance both from a regional and national point of view. Regional policies need to be geared much more towards promoting the industrial regeneration of the poorer regions by genuine job creation rather than by simply diverting jobs from more successful regions as in the past, providing of course that such a policy involves no detrimental consequences for industrial efficiency in general. Where the costs of job creation outweigh the benefits then serious consideration should be given to the alternative policy of encouraging labour mobility.

Given the high costs involved in moving employment to the assisted areas – estimated in 1980 at £30,000 per job[61] – it is perhaps surprising that more attention has not been given to promoting labour mobility. Assisted labour migration would clearly be much cheaper even with generous compensation for removal, while many workers might benefit from the opportunity to retrain in new skills and acquire higher-status jobs. The arguments usually put forward against such a policy are that it would deprive regions of younger and more skilled workers thereby reducing their attractiveness still further, that it would lead to a drainage of purchasing power and under-utilisation of the stock of social overhead capital, while at the same time adding to the congestion in the receiving areas.

Furthermore, the possible disruption to community and social life from a policy of induced migration tends to be a sensitive issue politically and probably explains why governments have given so little support to it in the past.

Even if the force of these arguments is accepted, we should not dismiss the need for 'a more fundamental re-evaluation of the role and shape of assisted labour mobility policy in the overall regional-policy programme.'[62] The policies of job creation *in situ* and labour mobility should not be treated as mutually exclusive. Communities, no more than firms or industries, can be regarded as sacrosanct in their existing form and, as Pitfield has forcefully argued, in the interests of optimal industrial location it may be necessary to consider the depopulation of a whole community as a real alternative to a policy dictated by social considerations.[63] While such drastic action would hopefully be a rare occurrence, there is certainly a need to improve the level of mobility to take account of changing job patterns in different areas and industries, and as a counterbalance to defensive actions aimed at preserving jobs in declining sectors and areas. Over a normal working life many employees can expect to change jobs and develop new skills which will often entail a change in work location and place of residence. Much of the migration in the past has been largely unassisted, at least from public sources, but surveys indicate that there would be a greater willingness to move if there was adequate compensation and better provision for retraining and accommodation.[64] The last decade has seen an improvement in the facilities offered in this respect,[65] but labour mobility as a viable alternative and complementary policy still needs to gain acceptance. Moreover, retraining and migration incentive policies need to be planned on a co-ordinated basis since otherwise retraining carried out in the depressed regions may prove worthless if not specifically linked with incentives to encourage workers to move to areas where jobs are available in their new fields of endeavour.

Thus there is considerable scope for a more constructive policy effort to assist workers to retrain and migrate, and to provide information about job opportunities in different areas. At the same time some of the institutional impediments which hinder labour mobility, such as housing policies and trade union restrictions, need to be modified in the interests of improving the operation of the labour market.

NOTES

1 For details see Chapter 1, and N. Bosanquet, 'Structuralism and Structural Unemployment', *British Journal of Industrial Relations*, **17** (1979). It should also be noted that localised structural imbalance within regions may have increased in recent years, especially in the inner areas of large towns and cities. In London, for example, manufacturing employment fell by over one-third between 1966 and 1976 and in parts of London unemployment rates were comparable to those of the North.

2 In the 1960s, for example, when a more vigorous regional policy was adopted, and possibly more recently as agglomeration diseconomies became apparent in the south-east.

3 A. D. Campbell, 'Changes in Scottish Incomes, 1924 – 49', *Economic Journal*, **65** (1955).

4 Regional Statistics, 1981; and H. W. Richardson, *Elements of Regional Economics* (1969), p.61.

5 That is in the absence of regional assistance.

6 S. L. Edwards, 'Regional Variations in Freight Costs', *Journal of Transport Economics and Policy*, **9** (1975).

7 D. I. Mackay, 'Industrial Structure and Regional Growth: A Methodological Problem', *Scottish Journal of Political Economy*, **15** (1968), p.139.

8 Richardson, *op. cit.*, p.57.

9 N. K. Buxton, 'Economic Growth in Scotland between the Wars: The Role of Production Structure and Rationalisation', *Economic History Review*, **33** (November 1980).

10 D. H. Aldcroft, *The Inter-War Economy: Britain 1919 – 1939* (1970), pp.90 – 8.

11 A favourable *industrial composition or mix* reflects either an over-representation of low redundancy sectors or an under-representation of high redundancy sectors, and vice versa. The *regional effect* represents the difference between the redundancy rate for the same industry in the specific region and nationally, weighted by the relative importance of that industry in the region. Thus a favourable regional effect occurs when the industry-specific redundancy rate is lower in the region in question, and vice versa. R. L. Martin, 'Job Loss and the Regional Incidence of Redundancies in the Current Recession', *Cambridge Journal of Economics*, **6** (December 1982).

12 See G. Gudgin, *Industrial Location Processes and Regional Employment Growth* (1978).

13 Segal notes that while the structural format of the poorer regions has generally improved, their supply capability in terms of small manu-

facturing firms and new technologies, and the development of an adequate professional capability in management, market research, corporate planning, R. & D., and other specialised professional skills, still leaves much to be desired. He attributes the poor response in entrepreneurship and professional capability to (1) the nature of the traditional products – heavy, large-scale capital goods of a highly cyclical nature; (2) domination of traditional firms, large-size, vertically-integrated and paternally-managed; (3) geographical settlement patterns – dispersed and largely self-contained labour markets each dependent on a single industry, or even a single employer. Moreover, the existing spatial configuration of resources and infrastructure facilities *within* a region may be inappropriate for a dynamic response. See N. S. Segal, 'The Limits and Means of "Self-Reliant" Regional Economic Growth'; and J. B. Parr, 'Spatial Structure as a Factor in Economic Adjustment and Regional Policy', in D. Maclennan and J. B. Parr (eds.), *Regional Policy: Past Experience and New Directions* (1979).

14 D. H. Aldcroft, *The East Midlands Economy* (1979), p.40.

15 Swales adds a note of caution about pressing this point too strongly since some of the evidence is conflicting. J. K. Swales, 'Entrepreneurship and Regional Development: Implications for Regional Policy', in D. Maclennan and J. B. Parr (eds.), *Regional Policy: Past Experience and New Directions* (1979).

16 There is no reason to assume, of course, that the division between poor and prosperous regions will remain exactly the same as in the past where the split between North and South was quite distinct. Indeed, the emergence of the West Midlands – once a very prosperous area – as a problem region in the last decade suggests that the pattern is changing, and at the time of writing plans are afoot to designate this region as an assisted area. See *Financial Times*, 1 September 1983.

17 Gudgin, *op. cit.*

18 F. M. Miller, 'The Unemployment Policy of the National Government, 1931 – 1936', *The Historical Journal*, **19** (1976), p.469. The actual number of new factories in England and Wales which did go to the four special areas designated in the 1934 legislation was very small; out of a total of 2058 between 1934 and 1937 only 34 were located in these areas, and 16 out of 764 expanded factories. The proportion increased somewhat after 1937 when the revised legislation gave the commissioners additional powers.

19 D. E. Pitfield, *Labour Migration and the Regional Problem in Britain, 1920-1939.*, PhD University of Stirling (1973), p.402.

20 H. W. Richardson and E. G. West, 'Must We Always Take Work to the Workers?', *Lloyds Bank Review*, **71** (January 1964), p.48.

21 R. Shay, *British Rearmament in the Thirties: Politics and Profits* (1977), pp.125, 134; G. C. Peden, 'Keynes, the Treasury and Unemployment in the Later Nineteen Thirties', *Oxford Economic Papers*, **32** (1980); R. A. C. Parker, 'British Rearmament, 1936-9: Treasury, Trade

Unions and Skilled Labour', *English Historical Review*, **96** (1981), pp.317-18.

22 D.Smith, 'Britain's Recovery: The Bottleneck Factor', *Financial Weekly*, 3 June 1983.

23 R.G.D.Allen and B.Thomas, 'The Supply of Engineering Labour under Boom Conditions', *Economic Journal*, **49** (1939), pp.264, 274.

24 *Department of Employment Gazette*, June 1974.

25 S.Constantine, *Unemployment in Britain between the Wars* (1980), pp.22, 26.

26 G.Hughes and B.McCormick, 'Do Council Housing Policies Reduce Migration between Regions?', *Economic Journal*, **91** (December 1981).

27 As Wilson has noted, the housing allocation criteria and pricing policies of local housing authorities have been anything but conducive to mobility. T.Wilson, 'Regional Policy and the National Interest', in D.Maclennan and J.B.Parr (eds), *Regional Policy: Past Experience and New Directions* (1979), p.93.

28 S.Glynn and A.Booth, 'Unemployment in Interwar Britain: A Case for Relearning the Lessons of the 1930s?', *Economic History Review*, **36** (August 1983), p.337, note 53.

29 Ibid., p.247.

30 In fact, at times real incomes have risen fastest where unemployment has been highest.

31 In the inter-war years the unions implicitly accepted high unemployment as the price to be paid for maintaining wage levels of those in employment. As real wages rose with the fall in the cost of living they became more interested in improving the rate of unemployment benefit than raising the level of employment since benefit support helped to reduce job competition which would have acted to depress wages. J.A.Garraty, 'Unemployment During the Great Depression', *Labour History*, **17** (1976), pp.137–8.

32 P.Minford, *Unemployment: Cause and Cure* (1983), pp.82–3.

33 J.M.Keynes, 'How to Avoid a Slump. Looking Ahead. I. The Problem of the Steady Level', *The Times*, 12 January 1937.

34 K.Hawkins, *Unemployment* (1979), p.64.

35 The strength of the regional multipliers has been the subject of some debate, but it is generally true that it is insufficient to ensure the restoration of regional balance. See Glynn and Booth, *loc. cit.*, p.340; and M.E.F.Jones, *Regional Unemployment and Policy in the 1930s: A Preliminary Study*, Department of Economics, University of Essex (1981), p.24; M.Chisholm, 'Regional Policies in an Era of Slow Population Growth and Higher Unemployment', *Regional Studies*, **10** (1976), p.202.

36 A.E.G.Robinson (ed.), *Backward Areas in Advanced Countries* (1969), p.346.

37 R.L.Martin, 'Job Loss and the Regional Incidence of Redundancies in the Current Recession', *Cambridge Journal of Economics*, **6** (December 1982), p.393.

38 In fact these areas are no longer major employment generators and the south-east has not been for some time, while in the past decade the West Midlands has become a problem region. The more favourable unemployment rates in the South are partly due to the low rates of demographic change as compared with the high rates recorded in the North and in Scotland. See *Cambridge Economic Policy Review*, **6** (July 1980); and J. R. Firn and J. K. Swales, 'The Formation of New Manufacturing Establishments in the Central Clydeside and West Midlands Conurbations 1963 – 1972: A Comparative Analysis', *Regional Studies*, **12** (1978).

39 K. Morley, 'Unemployment, Profits Share and Regional Policy', in A. Whiting (ed.), *The Economics of Industrial Subsidies* (1976), p.179.

40 D. E. Pitfield, 'The Quest for an Effective Regional Policy, 1934 – 37', *Regional Studies*, **12** (1978); D. H. Aldcroft, *The Interwar Economy: Britain 1919 – 1939* (1970), p.103; A. Booth, 'The Second World War and the Origins of Modern Regional Policy', *Economy and Society*, **11** (February 1982), pp.4 – 6.

41 *Cambridge Economic Policy Review*, **6** (July 1980), p.1.

42 By 1983 the reduction in the area eligible for assistance had probably been achieved but preliminary figures for regional spending would seem to indicate that it has not been contained as the Government planned. The out-turn for the year may be of the order of £800 million at current prices. See *Financial Times*, 1 September 1983.

43 Useful surveys of regional policy since the war can be found in J. D. McCallum, 'The Development of British Regional Policy', in Maclennan and Parr, *op. cit.*; and K. J. Button, 'Spatial Economic Policy', in W. P. J. Maunder (ed.), *The British Economy in the 1970s* (1980).

44 Some of the main findings are summarised in W. Nicol and D. Yuill, 'Regional Problems and Policy', in A. Boltho (ed.), *The European Economy: Growth and Crisis* (1982), pp.438 – 9.

45 Regional Policy shifted 1.6 per cent of the UK capital stock to these three development areas between 1959 and 1973. R. D. Rees and R. H. C. Miall, 'The Effect of Regional Policy on Manufacturing Investment and Capital Stock within the UK between 1959 and 1978', *Regional Studies*, **15** (1981), pp.420 – 2.

46 *Cambridge Economic Policy Review*, **6** (July 1980), p.36.

47 D. J. Morris, 'Industrial Policy', in D. Morris (ed.), *The Economic System in the UK* (1979), p.535.

48 For example, no attempt had been made to measure the opportunity cost of investing in non-assisted areas. See M. Chisholm, 'Regional Policies in an Era of Slow Population Growth and High Unemployment', *Regional Studies*, **10** (1976), pp.206 – 7.

49 Quoted in J. D. McCallum, 'The Development of British Regional Policy' in Maclennan and Parr, *op.cit.*, p.24.

50 G. C. Cameron, 'The National Industrial Strategy and Regional Policy', in Maclennan and Parr, *op. cit.*, p.320.

51 K. Morley, 'Unemployment, Profits Share and Regional Policy', in A. Whiting (ed.), *The Economics of Industrial Subsidies* (1976), p.179.

52 Quoted in F. Broadway, *State Intervention in British Industry 1964 – 68* (1969), p.116.
53 K. Williams, J. Williams and D. Thomas, *Why Are the British Bad at Manufacturing?* (1983), p.101.
54 Broadway, *op. cit.*, p.119.
55 C. Carter (ed.), *Industrial Policy and Innovation* (1981), p.230.
56 D. K. Stout, in ibid., p.123.
57 D. E. Pitfield, 'Regional Economic Policy and the Long run: Innovation and Location in the Iron and Steel Industry', *Business History*, **16** (1974), pp. 170 – 3; G. C. Allen, 'Industrial Policy and Innovation in Japan', in Carter, *op. cit.*, p.76.
58 T. Wilson, 'Regional Policy and the National Interest', in Maclennan and Parr, *op. cit.*, p.102.
59 J. N. Randall, 'The Changing Nature of the Regional Economic Problem since 1965', in Maclennan and Parr, *op. cit.*, pp.125 – 6.
60 M. Beenstock, 'Do UK Labour Markets Work?', *Economic Outlook* **25** (January/July 1979), p.30.
61 J. Marquand, *Measuring the Effects and Costs of Regional Incentives* (Department of Industry, 1980).
62 P. B. Beaumont, 'An Examination of Assisted Labour Mobility Policy', in Maclennan and Parr, *op. cit.*, p.78; see also M. Casson, *Economics of Unemployment: An Historical Perspective* (1983), p.251.
63 D. E. Pitfield, *Labour Migration and the Regional Problem in Britain, 1920 – 1939*, PhD University of Stirling (1973), p.402.
64 H. W. Richardson and E. G. West, 'Must We Always Take Work to the Workers?', *Lloyds Bank Review* **71** (January 1964), p.35.
65 For a survey of recent developments see D. L. Bosworth and R. A. Wilson, 'The Labour Market', in W. P. J. Maunder (ed.), *The British Economy in the 1970s* (1980).

6 The Constraint of Inflation

'Civilisation', observes A.J.P. Taylor in a recent memoir, 'can survive wars and slumps. Inflation destroys the foundations of society.'[1] Our present proposition for discussion is less ambitious but none the less important: that inflation destroys the basis for sound growth and employment. We shall be concerned only incidentally with the causes of, and cures for, inflation since our major interest is in determining the way in which inflation acts as an employment constraint. However, if the proposition is valid, then the control of inflation becomes a major priority and any policy designed to check inflation will involve, at least temporarily, some loss of growth and employment. In any case, once inflation appears to be getting out of control the authorities will feel obliged to take steps to contain it. Accordingly, we shall first look briefly at the effects on the real economy arising from measures to control inflation, and then proceed to analyse the ways in which inflation itself adversely affects the economy and employment which in turn justify action to restrain it.

THE IMPACT OF CONTROLLING INFLATION

The first point is the less controversial, and need not detain us too long. Let us assume that a decision has been made to bring inflation under control (to lower the rate) – for what reasons this decision has been taken are neither here nor there in this context – and that the authorities take the necessary steps to do just that. As a general principle one may conclude that if the anti-inflation policy is successful it will automatically generate an employment constraint since real output and employment will fall during the period in which the policy bites. Whatever type of counter-inflationary policy is adopted – be it monetary control, fiscal retrenchment or prices and incomes policy, or a combination of all three – there is no way of avoiding a real output crunch, except in the unlikely event of an instantaneous and uniform price response in all product markets. Defining inflation as the growth in nominal value of aggregate spending that exceeds the growth in real output then, as Gordon states,

any reduction in the growth of nominal spending, no matter how it is achieved, must by definition be divided between a decline in the rate of inflation and a decline in the growth of real output. The success of restrictive demand policies depends largely on the speed with which inflation responds to a sustained reduction in nominal spending growth. An instant and complete response means that real output is insulated from the policies. But a slow and partial response means that real output must take up the slack, with a resulting drop in production, accompanying lay-offs and unemployment, and bankruptcies of some individuals and firms.[2]

These nasty side-effects are one reason why governments are initially reluctant to implement counter-inflationary policies; and also the reason why, when such policies are instituted, they are diffused in order to lessen their impact on the real economy.

The adverse repercussions on the real economy are readily explained. When inflationary pressures are strong and self-sustaining – as in the 1970s and even more so in the first half of the 1920s in Europe – it takes some time to 'kill' inflationary expectations which are based on immediate past experience. Thus prices are slow to adjust to the new policies, and hence there is a lag before the rate of price change moves in a downward direction. Moreover, since during the period of downward price adjustment nominal spending magnitudes are being cut and pressure is being brought to bear on the major cost item in output – wages – it follows that at some point real aggregate demand will be falling. Alternatively, an unexpected reduction in the rate of inflation may have negative effects on the marginal profitability of output and employment, especially if output prices have lagged behind costs in the accelerating phase of inflation and if nominal money wages continue to rise for a time because wage-earners anticipate that prices will go on rising.[3] Ultimately a real output gap is likely to remain until inflation is stabilised at an acceptable level since it will be necessary to restrain nominal spending magnitudes and wage costs below the prevailing rate of inflation in order to roll the latter back.

In practice, therefore, it is virtually impossible to control inflation without generating adverse effects on output and employment. And indeed, the empirical evidence lends strong support to this conclusion since there are few, if any, instances of substantial inflation having been eliminated without recession and rising unemployment.[4] There are, of course, differing views on the real impact effect of stopping inflation and as to the type of approach that should be adopted. Some would argue that the responsiveness of inflation to a deceleration in nominal spending growth is quite weak with the result that the final real output effects arising from an inflation control policy may be quite large. If this is the case then the short-sharp-shock treatment to deal with the problem may be ruled out. Under these conditions a more acceptable and less costly alternative may be the 'soft landing' approach whereby a gradualist, counter-inflationary policy is consistently maintained which slowly generates favourable expectations about inflation. However, while under the latter regime the maximum shock generated is uniformly lower, it will of course last considerably longer, and the dangers of policy back-tracking are possibly greater. During the 1970s the second approach was the one favoured by most governments since it allowed them to 'minimise macro-economic misery'.[5] More recently there has been a tendency to tighten up control, particularly in Britain where the government has gone all out to defeat inflation regardless of the impact on the real economy.

Assuming therefore that the authorities react to public pressure to do something about inflation, then short of a miracle it is unlikely that they will be able to implement successful counter-inflationary policies without doing some damage to output and employment. In this sense, therefore, the control of inflation vitiates a full employment policy. At what point inflation becomes a cause for concern and requires

129

attention is a matter of some debate among economists. Some writers, for example, have questioned whether the real costs of control can be justified and have sought to minimise the adverse effects of inflation.[6] The opposite stance is taken here: that to allow inflation to go unchecked will in itself generate important real and financial costs which will impair the growth and employment prospects of the economy. In this context the frame of reference will be the inflationary experience of the recent past rather than the hyperinflationary episodes of the 1920s, the control of which, few would deny, was ultimately necessary.

CONSUMER SPENDING AND SAVING

It is not so much the absolute level of inflation which is the problem, except under very rapid rates of inflation or hyper-inflationary conditions when transaction costs mount rapidly, but its volatility which creates disturbances, particularly when price changes are unanticipated. In fact if all changes in price levels are fully anticipated and there are no significant adjustment lags, then in theory all costs, prices and price relativities in all market segments should adjust promptly and uniformly so that no sector or person is any the worse off than before; profits and incomes should be maintained in real terms and there should be no market disturbances to investment and consumer demand. It follows, therefore, that if the inflation rate could be determined or 'fixed' in advance, it would not matter whether it was at a rate of 5, 10, 20 per cent or higher since presumably it would be fully anticipated and all prices, etc. would be adjusted accordingly.[7] Thus a stable rate of inflation, even at a high level, may be just as acceptable as a zero or very low rate, provided it could be maintained at the same level from year to year since a constant, fully anticipated rate would be reflected correctly in the market place. Once there is any departure from this ideal situation the problems begin to multiply; as inflation accelerates price changes become more volatile and less predictable and unanticipated inflation whatever its causes, will produce uncertainty and confusion among economic agents whose disparate reactions to the problem lead to disturbances in the existing pattern of price and cost relatives and to a mode of behaviour which adversely affects economic activity. In other words, the greater uncertainty created by inflation reduces the efficiency of the price mechanism as a resource allocator and therefore leads to a worsening employment situation. Under these conditions there is little hope of any real trade-off between inflation and unemployment; instead inflation and unemployment rise in tandem and not solely because of the disappearance of money illusion (see below).

There are several ways in which inflation may exert a contractionary impact on the economy, and we shall examine in detail the influence it had on the two main components of national income, namely domestic consumption and private investment. The discussion will be illustrated by the experience of the last decade, though one should bear in mind that intermittent attempts to control inflation in this period also had an influence on the behaviour of economic agents.

Depressed consumer spending was an important factor in the slack economic conditions and rising unemployment of the mid-1970s. This can be explained by two related factors: an increasingly cautionary stance on the part of consumers in the face of rising prices and greater economic uncertainty which led to a postponement of new expenditures; and, second, and more important, a sharp rise in the propensity to save. Contrary to what one might logically expect, consumers do not readily spend their way into inflation to minimise the erosion of their disposable incomes in terms of product prices, at least not in the early stages of accelerating inflation. In fact at this point they are more concerned with the deteriorating real value of their savings and the need to rebuild these balances by saving more, a course of action encouraged in part by the lag in adjusting spending patterns to the rapid rise in nominal incomes, some of which is not regarded as permanent income. Moreover, the negative real interest rates which prevailed for much of this period meant that the savings effort required to restore the real value of savings was that much greater. Empirical data point to a severe deterioration in the liquid asset situation of the personal sector through the decade 1966 – 76, when net liquid assets as a proportion of personal disposable income fell to a low of 62-3 per cent as against 78-9 per cent in the years 1966–71. It is not surprising to find, therefore, that the personal sector's saving ratio rose sharply in the 1970s from 8.5 per cent in 1971 to around 15 per cent in the middle of the decade.[8]

Taylor has shown that this rise in the savings ratio was the chief proximate cause of the depressed activity in Britain between 1975-7. Taking 1963-6 as a base line, then actual GDP in 1975-7 was some $7\frac{1}{2}$ per cent lower relative to full employment GDP in the earlier period; had the net financial saving ratio remained the same as the 1963-6 figure then, *ceteris paribus*, GDP would have been 5 per cent higher in the mid-1970s.[9] Surrey confirms the view that the sharp rise in the propensity to save imparted a substantial deflationary twist to the economy – equivalent in his estimation to some 4 per cent of GDP. He also notes that if demand management had been called upon to offset the autonomous rise in savings through increased spending or lower taxes, an equally large increase in the public sector deficit would have been required which, in the precarious financial situation of the time, would have been out of the question.[10] The savings ratio remained high throughout the 1970s and edged up again at the turn of the decade when inflation began to take off again. Thus for much of the period the high level of personal savings tended to dampen economic activity. Subsequently, when inflation fell sharply after 1981, the savings ratio declined and thereby acted as a partial offset to the depression of the early 1980s.

THE PROFITS CRISIS AND BUSINESS INVESTMENT

The influence of inflation on investment and business activity in general is somewhat more complicated since there are several channels through which it may operate. Theoretically, inflation coupled with low nominal interest rates (negative real rates) should stimulate investment, not least because the move into real or fixed assets provides a convenient hedge against the erosion in the value of money holdings.[11] Certainly in the higher magnitudes of inflation, as experienced by Germany and several other countries in the early 1920s, the flight into

Sachwerte was quite marked, and for a time output, investment and employment were stimulated, though not always propitiously from the long-term point of view.[12] More recent experience suggests that this is far from being the case. Apart from the shift into property assets in the first half of the 1970s, investment, especially in manufacturing, has been fairly depressed for more than a decade. Of course there were factors other than inflation which depressed investment, notably external shocks including supply shortages, international recession and periodic policy measures to curb inflation. Nevertheless, it is also evident that inflation had a perverse effect on economic activity and business expectations.

In a general sense rising inflation created a climate of uncertainty for businessmen who found difficulty in coping with the new situation. Though inflationary pressures were persistent throughout the post-war period, for most of the 1950s and 1960s the rate of inflation had been low and fairly steady from year to year so that it was relatively easy to anticipate and accommodate inflation without undue disturbance. But the situation was quite different from the early 1970s onwards. The high and volatile rates of inflation were a new experience for businessmen and for various reasons they found it difficult to adjust to the new environment. The process of adjustment was complicated by two factors. First, price and profit margin controls were imposed intermittently during the period. Secondly, there was increasing real wage resistance on the part of labour as the money illusion of the earlier period disappeared. In fact, labour adjusted to the new situation more readily than capital and this is one of the chief differences with previous periods of strong inflationary pressure, for example, the Korean War, when labour had borne the main burden of adjustment. As we shall see, because business in the later period could not adapt fully to the new inflationary environment the consequences for employment were adverse. First, however, we must unravel the causal sequence of events.

The initial point of departure must be the dramatic collapse in profits in the early 1970s. While most series suggest that the rate of return and profit share in British manufacturing were declining from the later 1950s, they also indicate a very large drop in the first half of the 1970s. Between 1969 and 1976, the rate of profit on capital in manufacturing fell by no less than 56 per cent, while the share of profits in income declined by nearly 40 per cent.[13] According to Martin and O'Connor, the share of current cost profits in income of industrial and commercial companies was lower than at any time since the 1920s, while the rate of return was between one-quarter and one-third of that ruling in the later 1950s.[14] While some other major industrial countries also experienced a secular downward trend in profitability, in no case was it so pronounced as in Britain;[15] by the mid-1970s the rate of return on capital had reached miniscule proportions and many firms were facing a severe liquidity crisis.

The proximate cause of the profits squeeze was manufacturing industry's inability to adjust to the violent cost pressures of the first half of the 1970s. Initially these were mainly external in origin. Prices of fuel and materials purchased by manufacturing rose by 95 per cent between 1972-4 as a result of the commodity and oil price explosion and a 12 per cent fall in the effective exchange rate. In consequence the terms of trade of manufacturing industry (in terms of a weighted average of oil and non-oil primary product prices) initially worsened by about 50 per cent.[16] At the same time labour costs were rising rapidly as workers attempted to restore their real incomes, and the process of real wage resistance was accommodated by an expansionary monetary policy and institutionalised for a time by stage three of the incomes policy of the Heath administration which linked money wages to the retail price index.

The main problem was that manufacturing industry did not, and probably could not in the circumstances of the time, anticipate the sudden inflationary outburst. Hence final output prices lagged behind cost inflation and profit margins were squeezed dramatically. If industrial prices are cost-determined, then any price adjustment lag in output prices behind cost and wage changes as inflation moves to a higher rate will bring about a once-and-for-all profit fall, while accelerating inflation will produce a continuing fall in profits. Conversely, if final output prices precede cost changes then profits will rise. In the first half of the 1970s the former appears to have been operative since final product prices were slow to respond to the upward thrust in costs. Maynard has calculated that between 1972 (IV) and 1974 (IV) direct costs in manufacturing rose by nearly 59 per cent (a weighted average of labour, raw materials and fuel costs) while final output prices were raised by only 41 per cent, implying a fall in nominal profits of the order of 30 per cent.[17]

The question is, why were manufacturers so slow to respond to these cost pressures? One reason, already mentioned, is that they occurred rather suddenly and were therefore largely unanticipated or underestimated by manufacturing industry; in other words, a learning process is required before full adjustment can be made. Secondly, the cost-valuation policies practised by many firms may have delayed adjustment since temporary or self-reversing cyclical cost pressures will not normally be reflected in output prices. Thirdly, the traditional historic cost accounting and pricing methods practised by industry led firms to delay price changes until stocks of inputs acquired at lower prices were exhausted, though the problem of financing stock appreciation on a rising market should logically have encouraged the shift to a more rational pricing policy, especially as many firms were facing severe liquidity difficulties arising from the taxation of 'paper stock profits' before the introduction of stock relief in 1974/5. However, the elimination of the price cost lag may have been prevented by the severe price and profit margin controls imposed by the Heath Government, while slack market conditions after 1973 certainly did nothing to help matters.

The inflationary upsurge of the first half of the 1970s therefore placed manufacturing industry in an almost impossible situation. Given the deterioration in terms of trade, weakening markets and a lower rate of productivity growth, it was virtually impossible to avoid a profits squeeze unless the burden of adjustment was borne by real wages. But labour market conditions in Britain, unlike those in the US,[18] were not conducive to a fall in real wages, and in fact between 1973-5, own product wages actually rose.[19]

After 1975 there was a slow recovery in profits and by 1978 they had almost regained their pre-1974 levels. The terms of trade of manufacturing improved as a result of the abatement of external cost pressures, the beneficial effects of North Sea oil and a continuation of delayed adjustment in product prices. Furthermore, the growth of real product wages was contained in 1976 as a result of the effects of a new incomes policy. But before profits were fully restored in real terms, renewed inflationary pressures prompted a further squeeze. At the turn of the decade the nominal price of oil more than doubled, and manufacturing industry's terms of trade deteriorated by some 40 per cent thereby reversing most of the gain that had been made between 1975-8.[20] In addition, real product wages were rising rapidly since once again final output prices took time to respond.

What is particularly noticeable in both episodes of accelerating inflation is that the burden of adjustment was borne almost entirely by capital in the form of squeezed profits rather than by a compression of labour's income. The experience suggests that labour was much more efficient in adapting to high and volatile rates of inflation. Indeed, if anything, labour

TABLE 6.1: **Real Wage Gap in the UK (annual average growth rates)**

	Productivity (a) (1)	*Terms of Trade* (b) (2)	*Warranted Real Wage* (c) (3) = (1) + (2)	*Actual Real Wage* (d) (4)	*Real Wage Gap* (e) (5) = (4) - (3)
1972-75	1.0	-1.3	-0.3	3.2	3.5
1978-79	0.3	1.2	1.5	3.6	2.1
1979-80	-0.2	1.3	1.1	4.5	3.4

Notes: (a) Real GDP per head of total employment.
    (b) Income effects of changes in terms of trade.
    (c) Calculated as productivity per head corrected for terms of trade or the growth of real wage incomes consistent with initial factor shares.
    (d) Total compensation per head of dependent employment deflated by private consumption deflator.
    (e) Positive sign indicates shift to wage income.

Source: OECD, *Economic Outlook*, December 1980 and July 1982.

over-compensated itself with the result that in 1972-5, and again in 1978-80, real wages rose faster than warranted in terms of productivity growth and the shift in the terms of trade. The real wage gap (shift in income share to labour) that emerged can be seen from the approximate figures in Table 6.1. By contrast, manufacturing industry was never able to adjust fully to the disturbances, and so on balance its income share declined in the 1970s. Output prices lagged consistently behind costs, productivity growth was low or non-existent in some years, while real product wages moved against it. Summing up the decade as a whole Maynard writes:

the *ratio* of material (non-labour) input prices to output prices of UK manufacturing industry rose by a third, implying a fall in real value added attributable to labour and capital of about 20 per cent. Although, without some offsetting rise in labour productivity, a fall in own product real wages was clearly required, the opposite happened: the own product real wage rose by about 20 per cent. As a consequence profits were further squeezed, and employment in manufacturing fell quite steeply.[21]

INFLATION AND UNEMPLOYMENT

In both a direct and indirect sense inflation may be regarded as an important source of unemployment in the 1970s. High and volatile rates of inflation led to a serious price-cost adjustment lag at a time when real wages grew above the warranted rate; profits were therefore badly squeezed and this in turn depressed investment, output and employment. Two main employment effects may be discerned, first, a general shedding of labour as manufacturers sought to cut costs in the face of collapsing profits; secondly, a shift to labour saving investment as a result of a deterioration in the labour: capital cost ratio. However, it should be noted that in both cases inflation tended to intensify rather than initiate these trends.

As already noted, profits (both in terms of the rate of return on capital and as a share in total income) were falling in Britain – and in some other countries – from the late 1950s. Among other things this reflected an effort on the part of labour to improve its real wage position and hence its share in

137

total income. Paldam has calculated that in the major industrial countries the wage-income share, which had remained remarkably constant prior to 1939, improved on average by some 20 percentage points between 1948 and the mid-1970s. In the British case this represented a rise in the wage share from 71 per cent in the late 1940s (already high by international standards) to around 84 per cent in 1975. Conversely the share of capital in total income declined *pari passu*. However, about one-half of this change occurred in the first half of the 1970s largely as a consequence of the external price shocks and, unlike the position in 1950-1, wage-earners managed to pass on all the loss to profits.[22] Because of increasing resistance to real wage cuts on the part of labour, nominal incomes rose rapidly and with a flat or negative productivity growth this meant that real wages exceeded the equilibrium level to maintain full employment. It has been estimated that by mid-1975 average real wages were some 12 per cent higher than they should have been, while even two years later, after a restraint on incomes growth, the excess still amounted to 6 per cent. Subsequently, as the incomes policy disintegrated, money earnings rose at twice the rate of price inflation (1977-8), while employers' national insurance contributions were increased, so that once again real labour costs were moving in the wrong direction.[23]

In view of the intense pressures, it is not surprising that manufacturers were forced to shed labour on a large scale. Even if the profits crisis had been regarded as temporary, it was of such a magnitude as to shock firms into making a special effort to reduce their labour requirements, stocks, work in progress and investment.[24] Moreover, several studies have demonstrated that rising real unit labour costs and falling profits are associated with reductions in the level of employment.[25] Beenstock's investigations of the UK labour market, for example, suggest that a 1 per cent change in the real wage will eventually lead to an increase in unemployment of about 50,000.[26] Similarly, in a study on the relationship between profits and unemployment, Morley found that an increase in unemployment in one year was caused by a decrease in gross profits and the gross trading surplus as a percentage of GNP in the preceding year. He also found that this relationship was stronger and predicted better than either the net profits share of income, the rate of change in money wages or the rate of growth of real GDP.[27] More worrying from the long-term employment point of view is the possibility raised by Paldam that in some countries – and the UK in particular – the share of capital in income may have fallen to a level that is too low to sustain adequate investment and a full employment growth rate; for the mid-1970s he puts the latter at between 3-4 per cent per annum but which now would be somewhat higher.[28] If this is the case then the prospects for an early return to full employment look very bleak indeed unless something can be done to reverse the trend in income shares.

The second major employment effect arises through the capital substitution process as a consequence of a shift in the labour: capital cost ratio. Again, this was a continuation of a longer-term post-war trend. A combination of rising real product wages and generous tax allowances on investment meant that the cost of capital relative to labour declined, thereby stimulating a bias towards labour-saving investment. Though the substitution of capital for labour led to an improvement in the trend rate of growth in labour productivity in the 1960s and early 1970s, this was not sufficient to offset the rise in the capital-output ratio and so the gross rate of return on capital declined. However, the incentive to invest was maintained by virtue of the fact that the generous tax allowances on investment kept up the post-tax rate of return at a respectable level.[29]

If anything, the process of capital substitution was intensified by the inflationary upsurge of the 1970s, since real wages rose, labour productivity growth slackened, nominal interest rates were low and the allowances on investment were maintained. Thus between 1970 and 1976 the capital: labour ratio rose by 20 per cent in manufacturing but labour productivity changed very little.[30] Capital productivity declined as the capital-output ratio rose, while because profits shrank to very low levels the tax allowances on investment became increasingly irrelevant as a means of maintaining the post-tax rate of return. Under these conditions, though total investment declined the labour-saving bias continued because of high real wage levels and low or negative real interest rates.

Since under inflation real interest rates tend to be artificially depressed, firms faced with high real wages at a time when their product prices are lagging behind costs will tend to favour techniques which replace labour by capital. In this sense, therefore, the distortion of real wages and real interest rates tends to lead to a shortage of production jobs through capital shortage unemployment.[31] If this disequilibrium is not corrected then a higher rate of capital accumulation will be required to maintain employment, a difficult task at a time when profits are falling.[32] Moreover, continuing and accelerating inflation may intensify these distortions and exacerbate the capital shortage. At some stage, presumably, the inflation rate becomes intolerable and a firm anti-inflationary policy will be imposed. Since this will inevitably entail a rise in real interest rates and depress activity (as outlined at the beginning of this chapter), the extent of the damage to employment will depend upon the rate at which real wages can be adjusted downwards. This brings us conveniently to the question of real wages and the natural rate of unemployment.

REAL WAGES AND THE NATURAL RATE OF UNEMPLOYMENT

If, as indicated above, real wages are excessive and profits are low, then the solution to raising the employment level would seem to be a downward adjustment in the real wage level. According to Friedman, a high level of unemployment indicates an excess labour supply at the ruling wage level; this will exert a downward pressure on real wage rates thereby inducing employers to expand recruitment of labour. The adjustment process will continue until real wages reach a full employment market clearing level, at which point actual unemployment is synonymous with the natural – or perhaps better termed equilibrium — rate of unemployment.[33] The latter represents a position of stable and fully anticipated price changes, and the unemployment remaining consists mainly of frictional, structural and seasonal unemployment. Unemployment cannot be pushed below the natural or equilibrium rate without generating accelerating inflation; conversely, if actual unemployment is above the natural rate it may be possible to stimulate demand to reduce it provided that real wage adjustment takes place.[34]

Friedman's analysis of the labour market process raises a whole host of complexities, not the least of which is that of putting a value on the natural rate of unemployment. There is no reason to suppose that the natural rate will correspond to the full employment level of the 1950s and 1960s, though initially Laidler suggested that it might be of the order of 2 per cent. This scarcely seems a realistic estimate even for the period through to the early 1970s and, in any case, if correct it would undermine the basis of Friedman's argument that unemployment had been consistently pushed below the natural rate during this period. Whatever the natural rate may have been in the full employment era, for the more recent period it has certainly been a good deal higher given the increasing structural unemployment and the greater impediments to labour mobility and occupational entry in the last decade. In addition, in so far as the high and volatile rates of inflation of the last decade have reduced the efficiency of the price mechanism as an allocator of resources, there is yet further reason for suspecting an increase in the natural rate of unemployment. Hawkins suggested a figure of 3.75 per cent for the later 1970s which he regarded as being on the low side,[35] and a more realistic estimate for the current period might be of the order of 6-8 per cent.[36] But, as he points out, such estimates should not be endowed with too much significance, and in any case what is important is that even at the higher level, the natural rate of unemployment is still some way below the actual rate, as indeed it was in the 1930s. Even with a fully anticipated zero rate of inflation in the 1930s one could scarcely contemplate the absence of involuntary unemployment in that period; in fact, a natural rate of unemployment close to the prevailing rate of unemployment would have been nonsensical even to the 'most recalcitrant neo-classical economist of the period'.[37]

Even if it were possible to define the natural rate of unemployment precisely at any given point in time, it would not assist a great deal with the problems of adjustment involved in a high unemployment situation. Monetarists have devoted a great deal of attention to explaining the dangers arising from running the economy below the natural unemployment rate, but they have been remarkably reticent about precisely what happens, or should happen, when unemployment is above the equilibrium rate.[38] If, as Friedman postulates, labour markets respond to market forces in the conventional manner, then the excess labour supply will force down the real wage rate and the level of employment will adjust accordingly. One should note, however, that Friedman's analysis is based largely on the experience of the US economy where labour markets react more readily to market forces than do those of the European. On the other hand, Beenstock's recent long-term study of the operation of the UK labour market suggests that it is no different from that of any other market in which the price mechanism serves to equate supply and demand. His econometric investigation indicates that both the supply and demand for labour have in the past been influenced by movements in real earnings per manhour. Though the estimated elasticities are on the low side, they provide some support for the view that in time the labour market is brought into balance through the real wage mechanism irrespective of what happens to output. In a period of very heavy unemployment the process takes some time to complete, but short of a renewed dramatic disturbance to the labour market mass unemployment should not be a problem in the next decade. If the entire adjustment has to come through a real wage shift, the model implies little change in real wages through to 1987-8 as a result of the weak state of the labour market during a period of rapid population growth. Static real wages induce additional labour into employment at the expense of investment, presumably what would have been labour-saving investment. Then, by the end of the decade, when population growth levels off, the supply pressure in the labour market is relaxed and real wage growth can be resumed.[39]

While there seems little doubt that a compression of the real wage level would draw more workers into active employment, one can feel less than sanguine about the implicit faith placed in the market mechanism as a means of restoring equilibrium in the labour market. Moreover, whether, as Beenstock suggests, a static real wage level would be sufficient to bring labour markets into balance is questionable given the fact that it is assumed to operate independently of what happens to output. In any case, if the market mechanism does operate in the way postulated and equates the demand for and supply of labour at the natural rate, there would still be a large residue of unemployment since, as we have suggested, the level of unemployment at the natural rate may now be quite considerable. Because this type of unemployment is largely determined by structural factors on the real side of the economy, including various institutional impediments which hinder the mobility of labour (for example, housing legislation, union restrictions on occupational entry), it would not be possible to push the unemployment rate down further, that is below the natural rate, without generating more inflation. It is possible of course that as labour markets gravitate towards the natural rate, the latter itself will decline, while monetarists would argue that specific micro-policies are required to loosen the institutional constraints on labour mobility and transfer in order to lower the natural rate.[40] Short of such action the natural rate of unemployment is likely to remain high because since the early 1970s labour markets have become much less flexible and more segmented than they were in the 1950s and 1960s.[41]

A further and more important cause for anxiety relates to the feasibility of compressing real wages. Several doubts have been raised on this score by latter-day Keynesians, and Keynes himself, while acknowledging the fact that real wages could be excessive, doubted whether it was realistic to expect workers to accept a general cut in wages in order to reduce them. Keynes therefore favoured a general price rise above the rate of money wage growth as an alternative solution, which at the time seemed appropriate given the slack price conditions.[42] Such a course of action would scarcely be acceptable at the present time in view of the struggle governments have mounted to bring inflation under control. We are left therefore with the necessity of restraining or reducing real wages. This may be a more difficult task than most monetarists envisage, especially in an economy such as Britain's which is dominated by unions determined to resist the erosion of real incomes. At one time it was even thought that high unemployment would fail to depress the rate of growth of money wages, but recent experience would appear to invalidate this notion–there is always some level of unemployment at which nominal wages will be activated in a downward direction.

The compression of real wages is another matter however. The record with respect to a downward adjustment of real wages in recent years has been somewhat mixed partly because price inflation has fallen faster than anticipated, and partly because of strong real wage resistance on the part of organised labour. Moreover, as Minford argues, this resistance may be strengthened by the high minimum wage set by the government through public employment and social security benefits which the unions use as a base for a substantial mark-up for their own wages. This mechanism effectively limits the downward flexibility of wages. The minimum level acts as a floor under the whole wage structure and therefore wages cannot readily fall below this level even for the least skilled worker. 'It follows that shifts in economic conditions which would warrant a fall in real costs, will have only a limited effect on them and unemployment will result instead.'[43] The solution then would be to lower the minimum floor level by cutting social security benefits, which, according to Minford's estimates, would have a substantial impact on employment.[44]

It is interesting to note that a similar debate on inter-war unemployment benefits and the related issue of the real wage level has recently been opened up by Benjamin and Kochin.[45] Their analysis purports to show that a high benefit: wage ratio was responsible for a large part of inter-war unemployment. The arguments and issues are very similar to those of the contemporary debate, though of course they are set against a non-inflationary background.[46]

The failure of real wages to respond sufficiently to excess labour supply may therefore lead to a considerable volume of involuntary unemployment even when the rate of price inflation is fully anticipated. In point of fact the experience of the recent past suggests a less than fully anticipated fall in the rate of price inflation and the maintenance of real wages both of which have had an adverse impact on employers' expectations about the future level of profitability and hence on their willingness to invest and recruit labour.[47] Finally Wilson, recalling arguments used in the inter-war years, raises the possibility of the depressive effects on demand of real wage reductions unless offset by higher expenditure elsewhere, for example, public spending.[48] In the short term this is unlikely to present a serious problem, at least in the context of contemporary conditions since it should be possible to maintain consumption by running down the high level of savings and through the additional consuming power of those drawn into employment as a result of the decline in real wages.

The main conclusion from the foregoing argument is that downward real wage adjustment cannot produce a return to former full employment levels, though undoubtedly it will help to reactivate the labour market and draw more workers into employment. The difficulties of achieving real wage adjustment should be recognised, however, not least because of the strong real wage resistance on the part of the unions. The high floor or minimum to the natural rate of unemployment limits the scope for achieving low levels of unemployment without inflation by conventional means. Indeed, the success of traditional macro-economic policies in this context may be limited even when actual unemployment is above the natural rate and when the inflation rate is falling. If action is taken too soon to deal with unemployment the revised expectations about inflation (falling) may be frustrated; successive wage bargains will therefore anticipate a renewed upward shift in inflation and the whole process will start again. As Henneberry and White have observed: 'If policy-makers respond to the increased unemployment with expansionary measures before sufficient time has elapsed for the revision of inflationary expectations, these expectations will appear to have been confirmed and will thereby be reinforced.'[49] In other words, what is required is some relevant experience with price-level stability, a learning process to consolidate new expectations, and this may take some time to complete. As the authors point out, even Keynes recognised the value of some classical doctrine when he wrote in his last published article: 'If we reject the classical medicine from our systems altogether, we may just drift on from expedient to expedient and never really get fit again.'[50]

REAL WAGES AND CROWDING OUT

The real wage issue cannot finally be laid to rest until we have considered its relevance to crowding out. Versions of the crowding out hypothesis seem to gain in popularity at times when they appear at first sight to be least relevant, namely when real resources are underutilised. In the inter-war years, for example, economic policy was strongly influenced by the establishment view that any expansion in public sector activity would be offset by an equivalent reduction in private sector investment, while in recent years more elaborate arguments have been used to demonstrate the harmful effects of a large and growing public sector.[51] Opponents however would counter that crowding out is irrelevant at times of slack economic conditions.

In fact it can be shown that some form of crowding out, both real and financial, can occur at any level of activity simply through the psychological reaction of markets to changes in government policy. This is particularly true, as we have seen, on the financial side since markets react adversely to policy changes which they feel will lead to a deterioration in financial conditions. It is possible, moreover, for pure crowding out to take place at any level of unemployment under a regime of fixed real wages, as Mark Casson has recently demonstrated in his stimulating new work on unemployment.[52]

Casson's pure crowding out thesis between the public and private sectors of the economy rests on the assumption that the real wage level is fixed through the pressure of real wage bargaining. Thus any increase in product prices caused by a rise in government financed expenditure leads to a compensating rise in money wages as unions attempt to maintain their real incomes. Under these conditions the main consequence of any change in government spending will be a rise in money product prices; the supply of output remains inelastic with respect to price changes and money prices will rise until the higher level of nominal demand corresponds to the original level of real demand. Furthermore, the rise in money prices will tend to reduce the real value of government demand and at the same time encourage private individuals to increase their savings. In other words, when real wage resistance is strong, higher government spending will not be translated into higher output; it will simply crowd out private expenditure through higher product prices and the multiplier effects will be zero.[53]

While financial and real resource crowding out may be somewhat less significant in times of depressed activity, the existence of real wage crowding out has important implications with respect to policy formation at a time of heavy unemployment. If real wage resistance is complete then fiscal and monetary policy become impotent. To quote Casson: 'Once the real wage level has been fixed, expansionist fiscal and monetary policies will be purely inflationary: 'crowding out' in the product market will be complete, and the employment multiplier will be zero.'[54] In the short term there may well be a temporary stimulus to activity and employment from reflationary policies insofar as money wages take time to adjust to the change in product prices; but recent experience suggests that union bargaining soon neutralises such benefits by restoring the real wage level. Output and employment therefore return to previous levels and the level of employment is determined primarily by the ability of the unions to resist real wage cuts. It follows therefore that the government has little room for manoeuvre in its management of the economy unless it can permanently depress the level of real wages.

INFLATION AND THE EXCHANGE RATE

One final point worthy considering in this chapter is the relationship between inflation and the exchange rate, given Britain's heavy dependence on external trade and her poor record until recently on inflation. Conflicting objectives pose something of a problem with respect to exchange rate policy, which partly explains why the authorities have at times adopted a somewhat ambivalent and vacillating stance on the question. Since Britain has in the past had both high inflation and a weak balance of payments it has proved difficult to determine an exchange rate to satisfy both counts. A high exchange rate will ease the inflation problem but weaken the external account; conversely a low or depreciating exchange rate should, given favourable trading elasticities, improve the balance of payments but add to inflationary pressures.

Inflation may of course be an independent cause of weakness in the balance of payments. If domestic inflation is higher than that ruling in major competitor countries and the exchange rate fails to adjust fully to compensate for the difference, then UK producers will lose market share both at home and abroad, with adverse consequences for the balance of payments, output and employment. On the other hand, providing the exchange rate reflects the disparity in inflation rates, after netting out productivity changes, there should be little problem on the score of price competitiveness. Unfortunately, while over the longer term the effective exchange rate tends to adapt to shifts in relative costs and prices so that the real rate remains fairly constant, over shorter periods movements in the exchange rate can be erratic and sometimes perverse, while overtracking of the exchange rate in times of major disturbance has sometimes been a source of strain to the economy.

The empirical evidence for the recent past is somewhat mixed. For much of the 1960s, at least until the devaluation of 1967, the exchange rate was too high and hence it did not offset higher domestic costs and lower productivity growth in the UK compared with her major trading partners. Subsequently, through to 1975, sterling adjusted sufficiently – as a result of formal devaluation in 1967 and floating of the currency in the early 1970s – to compensate for most of the loss of domestic competitiveness. In the process however sterling slid very sharply, especially in the first half of the 1970s under the influence of lax monetary policies and a large balance of payments deficit generated by the oil crisis, with the result that it exacerbated the inflationary spiral through its effects on import prices. UK import prices rose very much faster than those of strong currency countries such as Switzerland, Germany and Japan in the 1970s, which meant that Britain had less success in controlling wages and prices than these countries.[55]

After 1976 sterling moved in the opposite direction though not because of any major improvement in relative cost

148

competitiveness; the main reason was increasing self-sufficiency in oil, and from 1979 the tightening stance on monetary and fiscal policy. Since the pound appreciated substantially through to the early 1980s it exacerbated rather than offset the deterioration in domestic unit costs and led to a serious loss of competitiveness. Thus profit margins in the traded goods sector came under severe pressure, especially after 1979 when recessionary conditions became more general. However, only part of the deterioration can be attributed to the appreciation of the exchange rate. In terms of relative unit labour costs, the competitive loss between the beginning of 1979 and the third quarter of 1980 amounted to more than 40 per cent; during that period sterling rose by only 18 per cent so that the greater part of the competitive loss can be attributed to the relatively higher rate of inflation in Britain.[56] Thus despite the movement of the exchange rate in Britain's favour in the last two years, it was clearly imperative to lower the rate of domestic inflation.

It is clear, therefore, that since the early 1970s exchange rate changes have been both large and unpredictable and this flexibility has not made it easy to maintain specific employment targets. In fact it may be argued that large and erratic shifts in the exchange rate are no more helpful to the management of the economy than high and volatile inflation rates, and in so far as the former are determined by the rate of domestic inflation there is every reason for counselling policies which ensure a relatively low and stable rate of inflation. Probably the worst of all possible worlds is that of a high and volatile rate of inflation which erodes financial confidence and leads to severe currency instability and exchange overtracking as market operators take fright and drive the exchange down below its true equilibrium level. Under these conditions the exchange rate becomes a source of inflation in its own right. This situation was common in the European inflations of the early 1920s and, as already noted, it was evident in the mid-1970s when sterling went into a free-fall causing financial panic. Fortunately, the decline was arrested by a reversal of macro-policies under the instigation of the IMF and subsequently by the impact of North Sea oil.

From an employment point of view it is important to

149

consider the price mechanism effects of exchange rate instability. These, as Zis has pointed out, are similar to those associated with unpredictable and volatile inflation rates.[57] Because of the uncertainty engendered by erratic movements in the currency the exchange rate becomes an inefficient signalling mechanism which will result in a misallocation of resources and/or a shift of resources to activities in which there is less uncertainty. This may involve a shift from traded to non-traded goods activity, where productivity growth and technological change are often low, involving a loss of employment as the economy adjusts to the new structure of activity. A substantial structural change of this kind, as experienced in Britain during the last decade, would also tend to weaken the balance of payments. Moreover, in so far as the exchange rate is tending to depreciate, there would be a feedback to inflation. As Zis concludes:

other things being equal, the adoption of flexible exchange rates in 1973 will have contributed to the increase in the inflation rate associated with any level of unemployment relative to the Bretton Woods era. In brief, then, exchange rate flexibility is of doubtful desirability, because the uncertainty associated with it is likely to result in greater inefficiencies in resource allocation.[58]

Exchange rates changes cannot by themselves act as a substitute for appropriate domestic policies, a point demonstrated by the differing experience of countries with regard to the control of inflation during the last decade. It is true that countries with appreciating exchanges (notably Germany, Switzerland and Japan) had a better record on inflation than countries (UK and Italy in particular) where the exchanges fell. However, it would be wrong to conclude that currency appreciation was the approximate or sole determinant of the better performance on inflation. In the case of the former group of countries, currency appreciation certainly eased the process of controlling inflation, but the strength of the currency in the first place was determined largely by tight domestic policies, the primary objective of which was to check inflation. Conversely, Norway and Sweden managed to reduce their inflation rates in the late 1970s despite some depreciation of their currencies. The British case provides some striking contrasts over time. From the floating of the currency to the mid-1970s the weakness of the exchange rate was partly a reaction to lax domestic policies, and this weakness provided an additional source of inflation through import price changes. The subsequent appreciation of sterling in the later 1970s initially owed little to domestic policy since it largely reflected increasing self-sufficiency in oil. Moreover, the inflation rate did not respond to the appreciation of the currency as much as might have been expected because domestic demand management was not maintained rigorously enough. Ironically, the latter was substantially tightened when the beneficial exchange effects of oil were coming to an end, and it then proved possible to allow the exchange rate to drift downwards without serious impact on the inflation rate.

This again points to the crucial role of domestic policy in maintaining firm financial discipline, even though this may for a time produce a real output and employment loss. Relatively stable inflation and exchange rates are more beneficial to economic activity than the volatile rates of the past have been . It has, of course, been argued on many occasions that sterling is overvalued and that devaluation is required to restore Britain's loss of competitiveness. We are not totally convinced by this argument however. While it cannot be denied that an oil-based exchange rate of $2.50 to the pound at its peak was far too high, one has to remember that it has since adjusted downward substantially and now stands at around $1.50, its lowest since 1976. Secondly, experience informs us that British exporters have not performed notably better when the exchange rate has moved in their favour, which is consistent with our earlier observations that non-price factors play a significant part in determining international competitiveness. It is worth noting, moreover, that efficient firms were able to maintain their export capability even when the pound was at its peak. Thirdly, a significant and one-and-for-all devaluation would not only reactivate inflationary pressures, but it would probably also slow down efficiency improvements and structural change in industry. Exchange rate depreciation is merely a substitute for supply-side deficiencies in the economy and as such will do little to raise the efficiency of British industry nearer to the margin of international competitiveness. Firms do not readily improve their level of efficiency when sheltered by a depreciated currency,[59] and the experience of Germany in the post-war period demonstrates that a strong exchange is not an impediment to economic success.

CONCLUDING COMMENTS

The relationships between inflation on the one hand and growth and employment on the other are complex and variable, and it would be wrong to suggest that there is a uniform association between them. While in Britain and in a number of other countries there has been a consistent positive association between inflation and unemployment, together with a negative relationship between inflation and growth, in a number of countries these relationships have been reversed. Moreover, as Tomlinson has pointed out, in so far as governments in more recent times have chosen to put the control of inflation as their main priority, then the former adverse relationships between inflation and unemployment and growth become self-fulfilling prophecies by dint of the very policies adopted to check inflation.[60] Nevertheless, despite these provisos we feel that there is sufficient evidence to support the view that inflation adversely affects growth and unemployment. Thus, while we would not necessarily subscribe to the view that inflation should be brought down to zero, we feel that the disturbances emanating from high and volatile rates of inflation should be avoided. Policy should therefore aim to secure a relatively low and stable inflation rate in order to provide sound conditions for growth and employment.

NOTES

1 A. J. P. Taylor, *A Personal History* (1983), p.260.
2 R. J. Gordon, 'Why Stopping Inflation May be Costly: Evidence from Fourteen Historical Episodes', in R. E. Hall (ed.), *Inflation: Causes and Effects* (1982), p.11.

3   See B. Henneberry and J. G. White, 'The Unemployment – Inflation Dilemma in Macroeconomics: Some Contradictory Aspects of Contemporary Theory and Policy', *Scottish Journal of Political Economy*, **23** (1976), pp.34 – 5.

4   Gordon, *loc. cit.*, p.12; W. G. Dewald, 'Fast and Gradual Anti-Inflation Policies: Evidence for Germany, Italy and the United States', in N. Schmukler and E. Marcus (eds), *Inflation Through the Ages* (1983), p.705.

5   J. O. N. Perkins, *The Macroeconomic Mix to Stop Inflation* (1980).

6   R. Bootle, 'How Important is it to Defeat Inflation? The Evidence', *The Three Banks Review*, **132** (December 1981).

7   Some groups may still suffer, for example, savers in fixed-interest bearing deposits the rates of interest on which are slow to adjust to price changes. However, this in a sense relaxes the assumption of perfect market adjustment in the above context. In the imperfect world building society depositors lost heavily as a result of negative real interest rates in the 1960s and 1970s, and since most building society savers are older people, and borrowers are young, it involved a redistribution from poorer to better-off members of society. J. Foster, 'The Redistributive Effect of Inflation on Building Society Shares and Deposits, 1961-74', *Bulletin of Economic Research*, **28** (1976).

8   P. Falush, 'The Changing Pattern of Savings', *National Westminster Bank Review* (August 1978), pp.47 – 8.

9   C. T. Taylor, 'Why is Britain in a Recession?', *Bank of England Quarterly Bulletin*, **18** (March 1978).

10 M. J. Surrey, 'The Domestic Economy', in D. Morris (ed.), *The Economic System in the UK* (1979), p.117.

11 This only holds true, of course, as long as prices are flexible so that final product prices can adjust fully to changes in costs thereby maintaining profit margins.

12 See D. H. Aldcroft, *From Versailles to Wall Street* (1977), pp.141 – 4.

13 By comparison the downward trends prior to 1969 were comparatively modest, 26 and 19 per cent respectively (1955 – 69). G. Maynard, 'Factors Affecting Profitability and Employment in UK Manufacturing, 1960 – 1978', in W. E. Martin (ed.), *The Economics of the Profits Crisis* (1981), p.213.

14 Martin (ed.), *op. cit.*, pp.17, 23, 27.

15 T. P. Hill, *Profits and Rates of Return* (1979).

16 Martin, (ed.), *op. cit.*; and G. Maynard, 'Why Oil Prices Must Fall', *Financial Times*, 23 February 1983.

17 G. Maynard, 'Keynes and Unemployment Today', *The Three Banks Review*, **120** (December 1978) p.14.

18 See J. Sachs, 'Wages, Profits and Macroeconomic Adjustment: A Comparative Study', *Brookings Papers on Economic Activity*, **2** (1979).

19 G. W. Maynard, 'Factors Affecting Profitability and Employment in UK Manufacturing Industry, 1960 – 1978', in Martin (ed.), *op. cit.*, p.199. Own product real wages are defined as the money wage divided by the the wholesale price of output produced by labour.

20 G. Maynard, 'Why Oil Prices Must Fall', *Financial Times*, 23 February 1983.
21 G. Maynard, 'Microeconomic Deficiencies in UK Macroeconomic Policy', *Lloyds Bank Review*, 145 (July 1982), p.8; see also R. Dornbusch and S. Fischer, 'Sterling and the External Balance', in R. E. Caves and L. B. Krause (eds), *Britain's Economic Problem* (1980), pp.63 – 6.
22 M. Paldam, 'Toward the Wage-earner State: A Comparative Study of Wage Shares 1948 – 75', *International Journal of Social Sciences*, 6 (1979).
23 K. Hawkins, *Unemployment* (1979), p.73.
24 As Pratten has shown in the case of an earlier wages explosion. C. F. Pratten, 'How Higher Wages Can Cause Unemployment', *Lloyds Bank Review*, 103 (January 1972), p.15.
25 For a cross-country analysis, see J. L. Gutierrez-Camara and R. Vaubel, 'Reducing the Cost of Reducing Inflation through Gradualism, Pre-announcement or Indexation? The International Evidence', *Weltwirtschaftliches Archiv.*, 117 (1981).
26 M. Beenstock, 'Do UK Labour Markets Work?', *Economic Outlook* (LSE), 25 (January/July 1979), pp.27 – 8. See also Pratten, *loc. cit.*
27 K. Morley, 'Unemployment, Profit's Share and Regional Policy', in A. Whiting (ed.), *The Economics of Industrial Subsidies* (1976), pp.159, 179. The fact that a reduction in gross profits was found to be a better predictor of increasing unemployment than a decline in profits net of taxes and subsidies would seem to imply that businessmen are confused by the unreliable and complex nature of fiscal policy with the result that they tend to 'treat taxes and subsidies as windfall losses and gains'. This, however, would seem to conflict with Maynard's view (for which see below) that the post-tax rate of return has helped to sustain investment.
28 Paldam, *loc. cit.*
29 G. W. Maynard, 'Microeconomic Deficiencies in UK Macroeconomic Policy', *Lloyds Bank Review*, 145 (July 1982), pp.6 – 7.
30 G. Maynard, 'Factors Affecting Profitability and Employment in UK Manufacturing Industry, 1960 – 1978', in Martin (ed.), *op. cit.* p.213.
31 See H. Giersch, '8-Point Plan for Escape from Stagnation', *Journal of Economic Affairs*, 2 (July 1982), pp.206-7.
32 C. M. Cooper and J. A. Clark, *Employment, Economics and Technology* (1982), pp.81 – 2.
33 The natural rate of unemployment is not far removed from the Keynesian definition, in so far as both assume that equilibrium is determined by the market clearing level of real wages at which point involuntary unemployment ceases to exist.
34 See M. Friedman, 'The Role of Monetary Policy'. *American Economic Review*, 58 (March 1975); and M. Friedman and D. Laidler, *Unemployment v. Inflation* (1975).
35 Hawkins, *op. cit.*, pp.71, 74.
36 Minford gives an estimate of 7.25 per cent (1.75 million) for 1979, subsequently rising to between 2 – 2.5 million as a result of a further rise

in unionisation, a fall in real tax thresholds and a rise in real supplementary benefits. P. Minford, *Unemployment: Cause and Cure* (1983), p.30.

37 J. A. Trevithick, 'Inflation, the Natural Unemployment Rate and the Theory of Economic Policy', *Scottish Journal of Political Economy*, 23 (February 1976), p.52.

38 T. Wilson, 'The Natural Rate of Unemployment', *Scottish Journal of Political Economy*, 23 (February 1976), p.105.

39 Beenstock, *op. cit.*

40 C. K. Rowley, 'Unemployment: Is Government Macro-Economic Policy Impotent?', *Journal of Economic Affairs*, 3 (January 1983), p.111.

41 F. Bernabè, 'The Labour Market and Unemployment', in A. Boltho (ed.), *The European Economy: Growth and Crisis* (1982), pp.184–5.

42 For an interesting comparative review, see P. E. Hart, 'Macmillan Revisited', *The Three Banks Review*, 138 (June 1983).

43 P. Minford, *Unemployment: Cause and Cure* (1983), pp.2–3.

44 The relationship between social security benefits and unemployment is a complex matter and has been the subject of considerable debate in the last two decades. Most writers would probably agree that the level of benefits does have some influence on unemployment but that the impact is relatively small. Minford, on the other hand, maintains that they are a major factor in the high level of unemployment. In a preliminary work on the subject he estimated that a combination of a 15 per cent cut in real social security benefits to the employable and a reduction in the union mark-up to its level in the mid-1960s, spread over three years (1981–4), would reduce unemployment in the UK by around 1½ million by the middle of the decade. (P. Minford, *The Problem of Unemployment* (1981), p.15).

In his recent and more substantive analysis of the problem, Minford argues that the level of benefits, direct tax rates and union power have a substantial effect on the level of unemployment. His findings indicate that a 10 per cent rise in real benefits would raise unemployment by nearly 0.75 million; a rise in the proportion of the labour force unionised by one percentage point would increase unemployment by 0.25 million; a rise in employer national insurance contributions by one percentage point would add another 0.15 million to the total; while a rise in the standard rate of tax by one percentage point would produce 0.05 million more unemployed. To counteract these effects he proposes setting a maximum to the benefit: income ratio, a rise in tax thresholds and child benefit allowances and measures to curtail union monopoly power, the combined effect of which is estimated to reduce unemployment by 1.9 million over ten years (0.9 million from the benefit and tax changes over five years, and one million over a ten-year period from breaking the labour market monopoly). The cost to the Exchequer would range between £2–3 billion a year, a not unmanageable sum on current PSBR targets (P. Minford, *Unemployment; Cause and Cure* (1983), pp.8, 20).

45 D. K. Benjamin and L. A. Kochin, 'Searching for an Explanation of Unemployment in Interwar Britain', *Journal of Political Economy*, **87** (1979).

46 Their work has been severely criticised by several authors in a recent issue of the *Journal of Political Economy*, **90** (1982). A useful and brief summary of the debate can be found in S. Glynn and A. Booth, 'Unemployment in Interwar Britain: A case for Relearning the Lessons of the 1930s', *Economic History Review*, **36** (August 1983).

47 A similar situation occurred in 1977 when excessive unemployment can be explained by a substantial over-estimation of the inflation rate – by some 10 per cent – by firms and consumers (R. A. Batchelor and T. D. Sheriff, 'Unemployment and Unanticipated Inflation in Postwar Britain', *Economica*, **47** (1980), pp.189-90). The authors work also confirms the view that variability in the rate of inflation and an increase in real wages contributes to unemployment.

48 Wilson, *loc. cit.*

49 Henneberry and White, *loc. cit.*, p.35.

50 J. M. Keynes, 'The Balance of Payments of the United States', *Economic Journal*, 56 (1946), p.186, quoted in Henneberry and White, *loc. cit.*, p.35.

51 See R. Bacon and W. Eltis, *Britain's Economic Problem. Too Few Producers* (1976); W. Eltis, 'How Rapid Public Sector Growth Can Undermine the Growth of the National Product', in W. Beckerman (ed.) *Slow Growth in Britain: Causes and Consequences* (1979); D. Smith, 'Public Consumption and Economic Performance', *National Westminster Bank Quarterly Review* (November 1975).

52 M. Casson, *Economics of Unemployment: An Historical Perspective* (1983).

53 Ibid., pp.79, 83, 249. When higher government expenditure is financed by taxation crowding out will take place not only through the price level, but also through the reduction in household incomes as a result of higher taxes.

54 Ibid., p.249.

55 See D. Higham, 'Strong Currencies and Economic Performance: Lessons from Germany, Japan and Switzerland', *The Three Banks Review*, **130** (January 1981), pp.19 – 20.

56 Ibid., p.22.

57 G. Zis, 'Exchange-rate Fluctuations: 1973 – 82', *National Westminster Bank Quarterly Review*, (August 1983), p.11.

58 Ibid., p.11.

59 With reference to ICI, it has been stated that 'For too long it has relied upon a depreciating exchange rate as a sort of backdoor subsidy to help it keep its head above water in the basic chemical trade, and as such it has been the bellwether stock for all that is bad in U.K. industry.' (Lyddon & Co., *Interim Report* (April 1981), p.2.)

60 J. Tomlinson, 'Why Do Governments Worry about Inflation?, *National Westminster Bank Quarterly Review* (May 1982), pp.6 – 7.

Conclusion – The End of Full Employment

After a prolonged period of mass unemployment it is clearly very difficult to get back to full employment quickly. The sheer magnitude of the problem – some 3 million unemployed in the 1930s and again at present – means that a very rapid rate of expansion of the economy would be required to re-absorb these numbers back into the active labour force at a time when the latter itself is still expanding. Against this background there would appear to be little prospect that spontaneous economic recovery could solve the problem. An element of recovery will undoubtedly follow the current recession but it is unlikely to be sufficient to break the back of the unemplyment problem. The strong natural boom of the 1930s took time to dent the unemployment total and even at the peak there was still a residue of nearly 1½ million out of work.

Unfortunately, the main alternative solution, namely a conventional demand management approach, does not offer a great deal of hope either. In the short run such a policy would almost certainly create new jobs, but it would very soon run up against a series of constraints and before long it would be necessary to reverse the policy stance with renewed adverse consequences for output and employment. These constraints, which would be particularly severe if reflationary action were taken unilaterally, could of course be diffused by various controls, but ultimately it would require an extensive network of controls on economic activity, not unlike the German situation in the 1930s, to stop the system from short-circuiting. On the assumption that a democratic nation would not be prepared to tolerate this outcome, the latter does not appear a

157

feasible alternative, and we must therefore return to the Keynesian approach and briefly recapitulate on the nature of the constraints.

During the course of this study we have identified four principal constraints which make it difficult to maintain a fiscal thrust for any length of time. These are the reaction of financial markets, the balance of payments, inflation and structural/capacity problems. They are all closely interrelated and the inherent weakness of the British economy means that they become operative sooner than would be the case in stronger economies. The behaviour of financial markets is crucial to an understanding of the system of constraints. Financial markets react badly to expansionary policies because, rightly or wrongly, they anticipate a series of nasty side-effects in the form of higher interest rates, rising prices, a deterioration in the balance of payments and depreciating exchanges. These expectations are not entirely misplaced however, since the weakness of the British economy means that it cannot respond readily to a large demand stimulus. Because of the structural and capacity limitations outlined in Chapter 4, the supply capability of the economy is very limited, so that any expansionary thrust would have a quicker and more immediate impact on prices and the balance of payments than it would on output. These consequences would be evident long before additional capacity could be brought on stream to ease the supply problem. Moreover, the nature of the fiscal stimulus, in the form of a general increase in public spending, would probably intensify the problems, not because of a crowding-out of private investment – though this too may occur if interest rates rise sharply to accommodate higher borrowing – but principally because the sectors most likely to benefit initially are those which contribute little to the balance of payments or productivity growth.

Financial markets will therefore do their best to frustrate any attempted reflation of the economy. And past experience in both Britain and France suggests that they have sufficient power to be able to do just that. Unfortunately, there is a dichotomy of interest between financial and industrial markets. Financial markets regard monetarism as the correct policy, whereas industry leans towards a Keynesian view of the world and hence reacts unfavourably to policies of deflation which spell depressed activity and low profits. According to Boltho, this division of interest generates an 'expectations trap' whereby 'the public sector frames its stance in the light of its perception of the short-run reactions of the private financial sector to policy changes, while the private industrial sector bases its longer-run spending decisions on how it perceives the stance of macroeconomic policies to be.'[1] Tackling the expectations trap could, as he notes, be considerably more tricky than coping with Keynes' famous liquidity trap of the 1930s, since it would require simultaneous policies to generate growth and curb inflationary expectations, and we might add policies to improve the supply capability of the economy on which growth depends.

One way or another, therefore, the prospects for an early return to full employment look rather remote. Even in the unlikely event of an absence of financial constraints, an expansionary policy would take some time to reabsorb the excess labour supply, and this would depend on the heroic assumption that capacity could expand fast enough to generate a full employment growth rate. Short of such miracles we shall have to be content with more modest goals.

All past depressions have been succeeded by recovery and there is no reason to suppose the current one will be any different. However, given the major adjustments required it may take some time before sustained growth materialises. It is important, therefore, that macro-policy should not frustrate the revival of the economy. While fiscal and monetary policy in the past four years may have been too stringent, there is scope only for a modest relaxation. This is because we believe that stable financial conditions, including a constant rate of inflation, are an essential prerequisite for sound growth and any departure from these stated objectives will jeopardise the prospects of real growth. A second major requirement is a healthy balance of payments.

Traditional macroeconomic policies cannot alone secure these objectives since they depend upon the efficiency of the economy and its supply capacity. One of the mistakes of past policy has been its neglect of the real side of the economy, or its supply capability. As Deepak Lal rightly emphasises,

The most basic revision of Keynesian doctrine required may be to bring back an appreciation of the continuing importance of product-ivity, profitability and thrift – factors which for too long seemed to have been denigrated by Keynesian modes of analysis. Demand management, Keynesian or monetarist, may be less important than replenishing the springs of enterprise which have been the ultimate mainsprings of the secular boom we have enjoyed since the Second World War.[2]

Although the Thatcher government has laid much stress on the deregulation of markets and the importance of improving the supply side of the economy, the record to date is hardly inspiring.[3] Briefly what is required is a much more radical shift of emphasis away from the traditional defensive measures designed to prop up old and inefficient sectors of activity towards positive measures aimed at promoting new tech-nologies, productivity growth and structural change. More specifically, Murrell has stressed the importance of providing positive encouragement to new firms which are more likely to promote dynamic efficiency than older firms since they are less troubled by the forces of inertia.[4] Such policies may not be politically popular – and indeed in the short run they may exacerbate the unemployment problem – but, as the Brookings Institution has recognised on more than one occasion, they are the only viable way of generating sound growth and employ-ment in the long run. None of the teams of the Institution surveying the British economy could come up with anything approaching a cure for the economy just by varying the macroeconomic policy instruments.

Success, if and when it comes, will have to occur in the micro-economic foundations of the economy where the problems exist . . . [Productivity and real wages were seen to be at the root of Britain's economic malaise:] full employment with stable prices and current account balance will not be achieved unless real wages growth is restrained or productivity growth increases.[5]

In other words, without a strong industrial and micro-policy geared towards promoting efficiency and structural change, no macroeconomic strategies, even a protectionist one, will succeed in stemming Britain's industrial decline, let alone reversing it.[6] In addition to a major industrial initiative, a more positive approach is required to improve the operation of factor markets, including measures to improve the allocation of capital to small firms,[7] raising individual incentives via changes in the tax system, policies to facilitate labour mobility (retraining, financial aid and housing) and to restore the price mechanism in the labour market.

Whether government measures alone can achieve a fundamental redirection of the economy remains to be seen. It may, as Professor Campbell points out, also require a more radical change in the attitudes of society: 'An economic transformation depends on the possession of more deep-seated attitudes and attributes than those more superficial ones which can be conjured up by government action alone.'[8] Whatever the final outcome, it is clear that we are not going to see a return to the golden age of full employment for some time to come.

NOTES

1 A. Boltho, 'Is Western Europe Caught in an Expectations Trap?', *Lloyds Bank Review*, **148** (April 1983), pp.10 – 11.
2 Deepak Lal, 'Do Keynesian Diagnoses and Remedies Need Revision?' in A. Maddison and B. S. Wilpstra (eds), *Unemployment, the European Experience* (1982), p.112.
3 Though see D. F. Lomax, 'Supply-side Economics: the British Experience', *National Westminster Bank Quarterly Review* (August 1982), for a more enthusiastic reception of the present government's policies.
4 P. Murrell, 'The Comparative Structure of the Growth of the West German and British Manufacturing Industries', in D. C. Mueller (ed.), *The Political Economy of Growth* (1983), pp.129 – 30.
5 R. E. Caves and L. B. Krause (eds), *Britain's Economic Performance* (1980), pp.11, 14, 19, 22. See also R. E. Caves and associates, *Britain's Economic Prospects* (1968).
6 See C. Carter (ed.), *Industrial Policy and Innovation* (1981), p.156.
7 Several ways to encourage new enterprise are suggested by M. Binks and J. Coyne, *The Birth of Enterprise* (1983), pp.76 – 8.
8 R. H. Campbell, *The Rise and Fall of Scottish Industry, 1707 – 1939* (1980), p.188.

Index

Arndt, J.M., 48

Balance of payments, 46-7,
  53-4, 55
Beveridge, W.H., 48
Budgetary surplus, 44

Capital shortage
  unemployment, 72
Capital stock, obsolescence of,
  70
Chamberlain, N., 43
Crowding out, 81, 146-7

Deficit financing, 46
Deindustrialisation, 76
Demand management, ch.3
  passim; limitations of, 81-9,
  158-9, 160; see also under
  macroeconomic policy
Depression, 20-3, 65
Devaluation, 30, 32, 33, 34, 47,
  77, 150-1

Economic trends, 22-7
Electronics industry, 73-4
Employment, 4-9; contraction
  in, 4-9; full employment,
  56-7, 156-61; industrial, 4-9,
  10-11; manufacturing, 4-9,

10-11; public sector, 10-11;
  services, 4-9, 11, 64; trends
  in, 4-9, 64
Engineering industry, 79-80
Enterprise location,
  determinants of, 97-105
Exchange control, 56
Exchange rate, and inflation,
  147-52
Exports, 15, 102-3; Britain's
  share of, 78, 79

Financial markets, 46, 52-3,
  158-9
Fiscal policy, 29-30, 31, 32,
  33, 34, 39; limitations of,
  ch.3 *passim*, 158-9; and
  structural adjustment, 80-9;
  and unemployment, 38-47,
  50 *passim*
Fogarty, M., 28

George, David Lloyd, 32; and
  public works proposals,
  37-40, 47
Gilt sales, 46, 52-3; buyers
  strike, 52

Henderson, H., 38, 39

163

Import controls, 30,56
Import penetration, 78, 79
Industrial Development
   Certificates, 113, 117, 118
Industrial policy, 85, 118-19,
   160-1
Industry Act (1972), 114
Inflation, 45, 54; and
   consumption, 130-2; control
   of, 127-30; and exchange
   rate, 147-52; investment
   effects of, 132-40; and
   profits, 133-7; savings under,
   130-2; unemployment effects
   of, 137-40
Interest rates, 46, 53
Investment, 64-8, 71, 132-40

Jobless growth, 70-5

Kahn, R.F., 39
Kaldor, N., 48; policy
   assessment of, 48-9
Keynes, J.M., 28, 38, 39, 109

Labour/capital price ratio, 71,
   139
Labour mobility, 105-9, 111,
   121; impediments to, 106-9
Labour Party, 32, 38; strategy
   for unemployment, 58-9
Liberal Party, 38

MacDonald, J.R., 43
Machine tool industry, 79
Macroeconomic policy, 157-61;
   classical, 30-1; devaluation,
   30, 32, 33, 34, 47, 77, 150-1;
   fiscal policy, 29-30, 31, 32,
   33, 34, 39, and structural
   adjustment, 81-9, and
   unemployment, 38-47, 50 *et
   seq*; ideological response to,

30-1, 42-3; and inflation
   control, 127-30; limitations
   of, ch.3 *passim*, 158-9;
   monetary, 29-30, 31, 32, 33,
   45; policy options, 33-4;
   proposals, 32; structural
   constraints on, ch.4 *passim*;
   see also under demand
   management, industrial
   policy and regional policy
Manufacturing industry,
   competition in manufactures,
   68-70; competitiveness of,
   77-8, 148-9; decline of, 75;
   dynamic growth sector, 63-4;
   inefficiency of, 78-80; labour
   costs in, 100; profits squeeze
   on, 133-6
Mechanical engineering, 72, 80
Microelectronics, 73-5
Monetary policy, 29-30, 31, 32,
   33, 45, 128

National debt, 45-6
Natural rate of unemployment,
   140-5

Oil crisis, 67-8, 134-5
Oil production, and structural
   change, 80-1

Prices, 22-3, 67, 134-5
Productivity, 66, 78
Profits, 133-7

Regional Employment
   Premium (REP), 113-14
Regional Imbalance, causes of,
   97-105; characteristics of,
   94-6; convergence versus
   divergence, 95-6; North-
   South differential, 94-105;
   regional wage differentials,
   100, 108-9

Regional policy, 109-22; aims of, 112; coverage of, 112-13; impact of, 114-21; limitations of, 116-21; policy instruments, 113-14; special areas legislation, 111; spending on regional assistance, 111-12

Scotland, 15, 102-3
Snowden, P., 43
Standard Telephones and Cables, 73-4
Staple industries, 15, 16, 102
Structural disequilibrium, 75, 84, 140, ch.4 *passim*

Technological innovation, 64-8, 70-5; and investment opportunities 64-8
Telecommunications, 73-4
Terms of trade, 67, 134
Textile machinery industry, 79
Thatchernomics, 31, 49-50
Trades Union Congres (TUC), 32

Transition theory, 68-70

Unemployment, ch.1 *passim*; age structure, 16-17, 18; cyclical, 27-9; duration, 17-18; extent of, 1-4; industrial incidence of, 9-11; long period, 17; natural rate of, 140-5; occupational differences, 16; policy for, see under macroeconomic policy; public sector, 10-11; real wages and, 70, 140-5; regional incidence of, 11-15, 16, 94; sex differences, 18-19; structural, 27-9, ch.4 *passim*; youth, 16-17, 18

Wages, real wage gap, 136-7; real wages, 135, 137-9; real wages and crowding out, 146-7; real wages and unemployment, 70, 140-5; regional differentials, 100, 108-9; wage-income share, 138-9
Watchmaking, 73